A–Z

OF

HARROGATE

PLACES - PEOPLE - HISTORY

Malcolm Neesam

AMBERLEY

Author Malcolm Neesam in 2019.

To my old friend Michael Hine,
in gratitude for his unceasing efforts to promote Harrogate

First published 2019

Amberley Publishing
The Hill, Stroud, Gloucestershire, GL5 4EP
www.amberley-books.com

ISBN 978 1 4456 9656 0 (print)
ISBN 978 1 4456 9657 7 (ebook)

British Library Cataloguing in Publication Data.
A catalogue record for this book is available
from the British Library.

Typesetting by Aura Technology and Software
Services, India. Printed in Great Britain.

Contents

Introduction

The success of my Amberley Publishing title *Harrogate in 50 buildings* led to an invitation to write a volume for their popular *A–Z* series on British towns and cities, and this *A–Z of Harrogate* is the result. As the invitation arrived shortly after I had completed what I regard as my crowning achievement as a local historian, *Wells & Swells, the Golden Age of Harrogate Spa, 1842-1924*, but with a few months to spare before the first proofs would be ready, I accepted Amberley's offer, and wrote the text over the winter and spring of 2019. Although some candidates for inclusion were obvious, others occurred to me only well after the task had begun, and a few were last-minute additions. I also admit that a few expected entries have been omitted, lest the choice became too predictable. Throughout the process of both selecting the alphabetical entries and writing them up, it was my hope that the final selection would provide the reader with something of the essence, or character, of the unique community that is Harrogate, and that as well as finding familiar and well-loved features, the unusual, the quirky, and sometimes the downright eccentric would also be brought to the attention of readers.

A

Advertiser

Regardless of whether we read the *Harrogate Advertiser* in printed or electronic form, and regardless of our attitude to the reports and comments it contains, there can surely be few who would deny that it is such an important facet of our democracy that its survival is essential. It was during Harrogate's 'Klondike Years' – that period between 1835 and 1849 when Harrogate got its railways, its gas and water companies, its Improvement Act and its Royal Pump Room – that its first newspaper appeared. This was established in 1836 by the splendidly named Pickersgill Palliser, who announced that his weekly *list of visitors to Harrogate* would, from September, be expanded into a full newspaper to be known as the *Harrogate Advertiser*. The success of this soon led to a rival paper, the *Herald*, being published by William Dawson, which first appeared in 1847, but within a short time printer Robert Ackrill bought the *Herald* from Dawson. Initially, these papers were published only during the visitor season, which ran from Easter to September, but in 1867 they became all-year-round editions. The *Advertiser* was a Conservative publication, whereas the *Herald* was Liberal, qualities that were maintained after the two merged in the 1870s.

Both the *Advertiser* and the *Herald* managed to continue throughout the difficult years of the First World War, with its acute shortages of paper, and after many changes the two papers became part of the United Newspaper Group, which included several newspaper titles. The *Harrogate Advertiser* has also been owned by Regional Independent Media, and was taken over by Johnston Press in 2002. It is now part of JPI Media, which publishes websites and regional newspapers across the UK. This was well after 1952, when the *Advertiser*'s printing works moved into a new building in Montpellier Street, which lay behind the paper's main office in Herald Buildings on Montpellier Parade, which the papers had occupied since 1903. To this day, the building retains evidence of an advertisement for the 'list of visitors' on its façade, although in 1991 the office moved to new and larger premises at Cardale Park, when it was opened officially by Diana, Princess of Wales. Always technologically advanced, the *Advertiser* had adopted total photo composition in 1980, which replaced the old rotary letter press, and rapid computerisation followed. Further changes came in 2012 when the paper became tabloid, and changed publication day from Friday to Thursday. The

Herald Buildings was home to the *Advertiser* and *Herald* newspapers from 1903 to 1991.

computerisation programme enabled the *Advertiser* to reduce its office size, and in 2019 it vacated Cardale Park and moved into premises in Grove Road. As the champion of free speech in Harrogate, the *Advertiser* and its sister papers should be supported by all who have the best interests of the district in mind.

The *Advertiser* staff in their new office in 2019. (Copyright the *Harrogate Advertiser*)

B

Bettys

Bettys was established in 1919 by Fritz Butzer, a young Swiss confectioner who arrived in Yorkshire in 1907 with the dream of opening his own business. By 1912 he had settled in Harrogate and changed his name to Frederick Belmont, opening the first Bettys tea rooms on 17 July 1919 at No. 9 Cambridge Crescent. The café quickly gained a reputation for quality and service, and soon Frederick was able to claim 'under royal and distinguished patronage' on his letterhead. A purpose-built bakery opened at Starbeck in 1922, followed by Bettys branches in Bradford, Leeds, and York. In 1962 Bettys, under the leadership of

Bettys centennial window display.

Frederick's nephew, Victor Wild, purchased C. E. Taylor & Co., a tea and coffee merchants with a number of 'Kiosk' and 'Cafe Imperial' tea rooms across Yorkshire. The Bettys Harrogate establishment moved in 1976 into its present building, which had been Taylor's Cafe Imperial. This had been built in 1900 by a Parliament Street pork butcher named Hunter who had acquired the old Hopewell House that occupied his neighbouring site. The replacement building was in a style of architecture that is sometimes known as 'Scottish Baronial', which for well over a century has provided Parliament Street with one of its most attractive buildings. The large plate glass windows are regularly dressed with attractive and cleverly designed displays of Bettys products, which draw crowds of admiring spectators, Easter and Christmas subjects being particularly popular.

Bettys Harrogate tea rooms include the spacious Montpellier Cafe Bar on the ground floor, and the Imperial and Belmont Rooms upstairs, all of which offer splendid views of central Harrogate and which are themselves animated by throngs of Harrogate residents and visitors. As to the regularly asked question 'who was Betty?' – alas, no definite answer can be given, although there are several interesting suggestions in circulation, of which the author's favourite is that the name derives from old Betty Lupton, the 'Queen of the Well'.

Bessie Bocquet's Burnt Buttock

The Greville Bath, named after its inventor, consisted of an apparatus designed to apply dry air at a high temperature to the whole body or to any separate part of it. It was formed with light aluminium cases of various shapes, which could be adapted to fit any part of the body requiring treatment. The inner surface had fine wires attached to the frame, which transmitted an electric current that created a dull heat that could be finely regulated. Temperatures of between 200 to 400 degrees Fahrenheit were usual, although 500 degrees could be reached if required. The body part being treated was protected from scorching by means of being packed in asbestos and swathed in lint. Harrogate Corporation took up Mr Greville's equipment with great enthusiasm, until 1903–4, when a dispute arose in respect of liability.

It was in 1903, during a course of treatment at the corporation's luxurious new Royal Baths, that Bessie Bocquet, widow of a London wine merchant, received a burned buttock during the course of a Greville Bath treatment, the interior temperature of the metal casing having reached 400 degrees Fahrenheit. Due to a combination of inadequate lint packing, and the temporary absence of the attendant, who failed to respond to the patient's cries as the temperature rose, the judge awarded the plaintiff damages of £250, a result the corporation considered highly damaging. Neither the company nor the corporation wanted to accept liability, and the town clerk advised the printing of a corporation disclaimer on tickets would not remove liability for the misuse of the equipment from either the company or from the council. It was clearly essential to keep adverse publicity to the absolute minimum, and by 1907 the case was resolved to everyone's satisfaction.

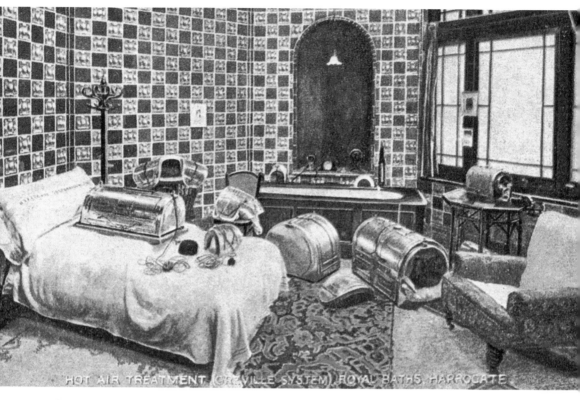

Above: Greville equipment in the Royal Baths.

Below: The Royal Baths main entrance *c.* 1929.

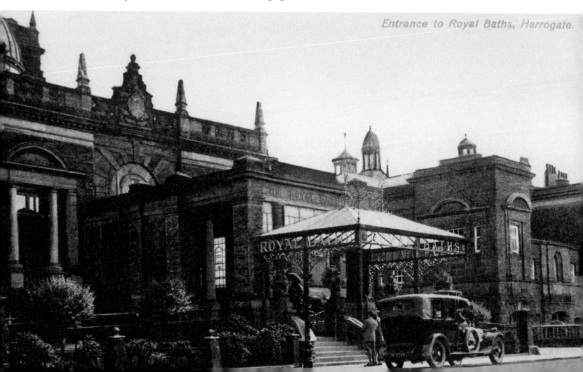

Cathcart House

Immortalised in A. A. Thomson's novel *The Exquisite Burden*, which tells the story of a boy's childhood in Edwardian Harrogate, Cathcart House stands proudly on Prospect Place as a large stone building isolated between the United Reform Church and Raglan Street. It was first listed as a house for the accommodation of visitors in the *Harrogate Advertiser* of 6 June 1857, which could indicate that it was built in 1856–7. Prospect Place's elevated location overlooking West Park Stray, its long garden frontages and broad footpaths led to the locality being nicknamed 'the front' as a possibly sarcastic reference to seaside attractions – or lack of them! From the start of its role as a place where visitors could be lodged, Cathcart House attracted only the most superior type of guest, an attribute that attracted the attention of an official of the Court of Princess Alix of Hesse, who recommended it to the princess, who wanted to visit Harrogate for treatment at the famous Baths. Princess Alix first visited Harrogate in 1894, when she stayed at Cathcart House as a guest of the Allen family, an experience she enjoyed so much that she offered to be God Mother to the Allen's newly born twins, whose christening service was held at St Peter's Church. Shortly afterwards, Princess Alix married the Emperor of Russia, Nicholas II, thus becoming Empress of all the Russias. As well as presenting the Allen twins with handsome christening presents, Empress Alix sent them gifts regularly, the last ones being for their twenty-first birthdays in 1915. Two years later, she was murdered by the Bolsheviks, along with the rest of the Russian Imperial family.

Princess Alix often spoke of Cathcart House to her family circle, including Princess Victoria, the sister of King George V, who regularly visited Harrogate in company with her cousin, Her Imperial Highness Maria Georgievna, Grand Duchess George of Russia. On 19 August 1911 Princess Victoria gave a little tea party at Cathcart House for her friends. On that day of dazzling sunshine, at the height of an equally brilliant social season, there was at Cathcart House a gathering assembled in Harrogate, the like of which had never before been seen. As the stately motor cars and carriages drew up before the building, they discharged the Queen-Empress Alexandra, Her Imperial Majesty the Dowager Empress of Russia, Her Imperial Highness Grand Duchess George of Russia, His Majesty the King of Portugal, Her Majesty Queen Amelia of Portugal,

Above left: Princess Alix first visited Harrogate in 1894.

Above right: Cathcart House.

Her Royal Highness Princess Xenia, Her Royal Highness Princess Nina, His Royal Highness Prince Christopher of Greece, His Royal Highness Prince Oblensky, the Marchioness of Ripon, Lord Derby, Baron and Baroness de Stoeckl, Miss de Stoeckl, the Honourable Charlotte Knollys, the Honourable Blanche Lascelles, Countess Heiden, Sir Reginald Lister, Major Philips, and Count Galvios. The Allen family, who owned Cathcart House, naturally wished the tea party to proceed smoothly, so they brought in extra staff from other establishments to assist their own staff. One of these, it was later told, was placed near the door with the main receptionist to take and label any items deposited by guests, and she was so overcome by the arrival of so many illustrious personages that when a further distinguished-looking lady entered, she exclaimed 'I suppose this is the Empress of India', which was overheard by another newly arrived guest, Baron de Stoeckl, who whispered kindly, 'No my dear, that is the Dowager the Empress of Russia. The Empress of India is in the next carriage.'

Chapel

In a town like Harrogate, with such strong connections to the Methodist movement, it is hardly surprising that at the height of the Victorian mania for building there were many places in the town known as the chapel, according to where one lived or which branch of nonconformity was followed. Today however, the words 'The Chapel' usually refer to only one place, which within the space of a few months rose to become famous not only in Harrogate but throughout the nation, and, increasingly, is becoming known to a global community of discerning travellers and film makers. To call 'The Chapel' an art gallery, a guest house, or a bed and breakfast establishment would be like calling Claridges or the Ritz lodging houses. The Chapel is altogether unique, and came into being in the following way.

When the urbanisation of the Grove Road locality occurred in the last quarter of the nineteenth century, the local Methodists built a school in 1892, the success of which encouraged the building of a large chapel on an adjoining site as their place of worship. The commission went to celebrated Yorkshire architect W. J. Morley, whose superb Italian Renaissance design was executed from 1896–7. The resulting monumental pile was enriched with magnificent woodwork, dazzling stained glass by Lazenby of Bradford, and a galleried place of assembly that accommodated 700 people. But when congregations dwindled, the pragmatic trustees transferred to

The chapel in Grove Road. (Copyright Alex Telfer)

Mark Hinchliffe in the chapel's main atrium. (Copyright Alex Telfer)

a smaller home, and the building, together with the attached school, were acquired by art connoisseur and businessman Mark Hinchliffe, who converted the former school into apartments before transforming the former chapel into a home for himself and family, and a place to exhibit his phenomenal collection of world art. This visionary task was completed in 2017, the painstaking work of restoration receiving regular coverage by the interested media, including much attention from the makers of TV programmes. Today, the former spacious balcony includes a series of spectacular rooms that are available for hire to guests from all over the world, as The Chapel is an exclusive place for receptions, weddings, parties, corporate hospitality, meetings and bed and breakfast accommodation. The spectacular success of Mark Hinchliffe's glorious creation is why, today, the words 'The Chapel' mean only one thing.

Harrogate Club

Today, the Harrogate Club is probably the most aspirational address in Harrogate, especially after membership reached and exceeded the all-time greatest total of 200, making essential the introduction of an upper limit. Founded in 1857 on Devonshire Place, the Harrogate Club, long known familiarly as 'The Club' was set up as a place for the town's professional classes to meet, read newspapers, etc., and keep one another informed about all matters relating to Harrogate. Naturally, the spirit of conviviality and friendship soon became central to 'The Club's' running, and although such well-established activities as dining and snooker are still popular, business networking is much more in evidence, particularly after the whole building was made Wi-Fi friendly, and the visitor is now more likely to encounter twenty/thirty year olds with smartphones and laptops than the traditional image of the older 'clubman' of yesteryear. And in any case, the Harrogate Club is more a 'club person's' establishment, as the rising number of female members and guests provides an atmosphere of

The superb snooker room at the Harrogate Club. (Copyright the Harrogate Club)

progress and innovation – and certainly it is this author's opinion that the level of conversation has been vastly enhanced by the growing numbers of lady members.

In 2014, the Harrogate Club began to plan a comprehensive programme of refurbishment, which covered every part of the magnificent mansion built for 'The Club' by the Bown brothers in 1886 at No. 36 Victoria Avenue. The basement, originally home to the club's steward and more recently leased to a financial adviser's business, has been beautifully restored to provide work stations for those club members who like to run small businesses from such a prestigious address. The roof has been repaired and strengthened, and the first-floor lounge with its neighbouring bar were restored and decorated in 2017–18 to such a high degree as to set the most exclusive standards for the restoration of the rest of the building. At the time of writing the dining room is being prepared for an elaborate scheme of refurbishment due to be completed by the autumn of 2019, costing over £60,000. The completion of this will then leave only the entrance hall, downstairs bar and the great Reading Room requiring refurbishment, which will begin in 2020.

Distinguished visitors Viscount Gormanston, Edward Fox OBE, and Viscountess Gormanston with members at the Harrogate Club. (Copyright the Harrogate Club)

C Is for Perfect Pub!

Our expectations of what makes the perfect pub are often shaped by the media – but how rarely does the reality match the carefully crafted image. How often does the customer have expectations raised by one aspect of a pub's service, only to be let down by another. We have all had this experience at some time. A pub has a delightful interior, let down by cold draughts from the mountains of Greenland. The food is wonderful but the beer tastes like flat dishwater. The beer is well kept and expertly served, but the atmosphere is ruined by intrusive background music. Sometimes one encounters a pub that would be perfect were it not that either the customers are too loud or the landlord too quiet. But very occasionally, the perfect pub is found, and as this writer has identified what for him is Harrogate's finest pub, he intends to keep its name to himself, lest it be spoiled by overcrowding! Maybe you can guess where it is?

Ideally located overlooking Harrogate's wonderful Stray, my perfect Harrogate pub hasn't changed much internally over the decades I have known it. It has never needed to change. Never needed the feverish makeovers that have ruined so many once-attractive pubs and hotels. My pub's interior has a warm and welcoming look, and if this look may seem a bit worn, the wear is the result of regular usage by

(Copyright Mike Hine)

appreciative customers. My pub's beer menu is the finest I have encountered, and clearly listed on the menu, which changes with the regularity that only a free house can provide. In summer the lighter beers predominate, whereas in colder weather the menu may offer superb and chocolately, rich stouts and porters. And despite the generous selection, the beers are always stored and served to perfection. As for the catering – words nearly fail me, as some of the best meals I have consumed *anywhere* have been consumed here (I must break from my eulogy to recall one rabbit and chicken pie, served under a golden dome of short pastry, and accompanied by an emerald mass of shredded cabbage, with mashed potato of the creamiest texture that positively soaked up the rich dark gravy, that was so superlatively enjoyable as to bring tears to my eyes). But to return to my text... be they vegetarian or meat dishes, my invariable response is to regret that I cannot dine here every day.

Thanks to the Nelson family (who have held my perfect pub for many decades) and their quietly efficient staff, my perfect Harrogate pub is both a delight to visit and a refuge from what can be a trying world. Opened originally in around 1830 on the old turnpike road for coaches and horses between Leeds and Ripon, it has survived the motor car and the rise and fall of the spa. Its future is secure.

Samantha and John Nelson – the proud proprietors.

D

Dawson, George

George Dawson was born in the village of Skelton-on-Ure on 12 June 1821 and moved to Harrogate in the 1850s, where he established himself as a cooper. He prospered through a mixture of hard work and obstinacy, and eventually earned enough to speculate as a builder, especially after he acquired the Ashfield House estate on Lower Montpellier Parade between 1862 and 1865. From then on, there was no holding him, and, as his biographer Bill Richardson has observed, 'in a town noted for its building, no other individual had the courage to develop on the scale he set, to approach the high standards of architectural design and building construction he demanded, or the obstinacy to go against authority and popularity to pursue the course he knew was right'.

Noted as a powerful lay-preacher, he was once credited with man handling a drunken member of his audience out of the hall, yet when he joined the Board of the Improvement Commissioners, he was on occasion called a hectoring bully! As a Commissioner, he was frequently at loggerheads with his colleagues, and broke

George Dawson.

the planning laws with alarming frequency, yet the results were so splendid that he gained widespread respect for the nobility of his vision.

More than any other of his colleagues, George Dawson shaped the layout and architectural appearance of central Harrogate, stamping his will on the town's ground plan in granite and marble. After Montpellier Parade, he created the splendid Crown Hotel extensions, much of Swan Road, James Street, and Parliament Street, and above all, the two magnificent structures of Cambridge Crescent and Prospect Crescent that still dominate the heart of Harrogate. His brilliant business instinct made him a rich man, and it was with a nice sense of humour that he named his Victoria Avenue mansion 'Vanderbilt Court', after the famous American financier. By 1889 he was in line for the role of mayor, following Nicholas Carter and Richard Ellis, but ill health prevented him from taking up the honour, and he died on 22 February 1889. A family man who was deeply loved, George Dawson earned the respect of an entire community for his achievements, and at his funeral service during a violent thunderstorm on 28 February 1889, the vicar described him as a man of extraordinary gifts with a palatial mind and great depth of tenderness as a person. His legacy, much of which was designed by the great architect J. H. Hirst of Bristol, will last as long as Harrogate values great architecture. It was appropriate that in November 1891 Webber's bust of George Dawson was exhibited at the Royal Academy exhibition in London, before being presented to Harrogate Corporation, who are still its custodians.

Prospect Crescent and James Street.

E

Ellis, Richard

Undoubtedly one of Harrogate's greatest citizens, and one who came to be held in such high regard that he was known as 'the Bismarck of Harrogate', Richard Ellis was born in November 1820 as the son of a High Harrogate Blacksmith. He began his working life as an apprentice joiner and cabinetmaker, but by 1849 had gone into business for himself as a builder, his first contract being for the New Inn on Skipton Road, known later as the Dragon. Ellis went on to build extensively on Queen Parade, York Place, Station Parade, and James Street, his buildings being of high structural quality and architectural excellence.

Typical Ellis villas on York Place.

Elected to the Board of the Improvement Commissioners in April 1855, he soon became a keen promoter of improvements in public health, voting reform, spa development, and long-term investment in the town's infrastructure. A devoted member of the Methodist circuit, he supported – at no small personal expense – church building, such as the first James Street Methodist Chapel of 1851, and its splendid successor, the Victoria Park Methodist Church of 1864–5, which he endowed generously.

One of Ellis' greatest achievements occurred in 1860, when with three other businessmen he founded the Victoria Park Company with the express purpose of joining the two ancient villages of High and Low Harrogate into a single modern borough. Ellis played a key role in overcoming the problems of introducing the new railway connection to central Harrogate, by negotiating with the Duchy of Lancaster an exchange of land whereby the land lost by the railway cutting across South Stray would be compensated by adding to the Stray the land occupied by the redundant Brunswick Station.

Ellis was also the key figure in the building of Ashville College, opened by him in 1877, and the whole town knew of his regular moral and financial support for the Harrogate Infirmary, his name being on the foundation stone laid in 1882. During the row over lack of road access from High Harrogate to the 1862 railway station, it was Ellis who succeeded in constructing East Parade as a solution, which was opened by Mrs Ellis in 1875.

Ellis' support for the building of the New Victoria Baths caused him to lose his seat, following his laying of the foundation stone in 1871, but he was soon returned when the public came to realise the value of Ellis' public service and expertise. The great success of the Victoria Baths was testimony to the soundness of Ellis' judgement. He was one of the greatest supporters of Harrogate's bid for a Charter of Incorporation,

Above left: New Victoria Baths *c.* 1909.

Above right: Richard Ellis by Thomas Holroyd. (Reproduced courtesy of the Mercer Art Gallery)

and when it arrived in 1884, he served as mayor from 1884 to 1887, following Charter Mayor Robert Ackrill, and the first full mayor, Nicholas Carter in that office. The councillors' splendid robes of office were presented by Ellis to demonstrate that the decorative embellishments of Incorporation need not be at public expense.

Queen Victoria's Golden Jubilee in 1887 was occasion for Ellis to present Harrogate with the splendid monument to the Queen, which he paid for in its entirety, donating the land as an additional gift. In contrast with some other members of the commissioners and council, Ellis was mild and softly spoken, given to humorous or kindly asides, and seems to have seldom been rattled by his opponents' hostility or malice. The address presented by the council to Ellis on 23 June 1887 referred to Ellis' unstinting service as chairman of the Improvement Commissioners, mayor of Harrogate, chairman of the Board of Guardians, chairman of the Pannal School Board, as a magistrate and as a supporter of a great number of religious, educational and commercial institutions: 'your labours having been so unremitting as often to cause anxiety to your friends'. Even in an age notable for the number of public benefactors, Ellis' devotion to Harrogate must be classed as outstanding. He died on 21 August 1895, his last public service being to support and encourage the building of the Royal Baths, to secure Harrogate's position as the leading spa and health resort.

Empire Buildings

Few buildings in Harrogate have had a greater range of uses than Empire Buildings, which at the time of writing is home to the popular Asian restaurant Cardamom Black, situated opposite Harrogate Theatre, at the junction of Cheltenham and Mount Parades. Although the name 'Empire Buildings' comes from the time between 1911 and 1931 when it contained the Empire Music Hall, it was built in 1872 as a chapel for

Empire
Buildings,
home to

the Primitive Methodists. Architect Arthur Hiscoe used Italian Renaissance elements in his design, which accommodated 450 worshippers, and included a schoolroom, a minister's vestry and a chapel-keeper's house. The overall cost for this handsome addition to Harrogate's townscape was £2,000. However, the increasing size of the town's population and the growing number of worshippers meant that by 1900, the congregation had to move into a larger chapel at the junction of Dragon Parade and Bower Road, and in 1901, the former chapel was acquired by Amos Chippindale, who converted it into a Friendly Societies Hall, with associated billiards room.

Theatrical entrepreneur and celebrated puppeteer James Holden opened his Empire Theatre on 22 February 1911, the surviving and rather magnificent proscenium arch having been carved by him. During the Empire's twenty-year life, many of the nation's most famous music hall artistes appeared here, and the screening of films – both silent and 'talkies' – were an additional popular attraction. Following the Empire's closure on 10 October 1931, at the height of the terrible Great Depression, the building became neglected, and by 1940 was in danger of collapse until it was bought by a remarkable German immigrant, Fridel Meyer, who recognised its architectural and historical worth and determined to save it. Fridel had moved to England from Bavaria in 1933, her first action being to get to know her new country, which she did by undertaking a solo 2,500-mile circumnavigation of the island of Britain by kayak, accompanied only by her little pet chow. By the time of her death in 1983, Fridel and her husband Glen had ensured the future of Empire Buildings by using it to run Blean's Toy Shop. But in 1976 after restaurateurs Tony Peral and Raymond Sandever opened 'Pinocchio's', the future of Empire Buildings as a restaurant was assured. Following Glenn Dalling-Hay's death in 2001, Empire Buildings was eventually sold, and Asian restuarant Cardamom Black opened here in 2011.

Cardamom Black's fascinating interior recalls a theatrical history. (Courtesy of Nick Rahmon)

F

Fat Badger

Although the Fat Badger is not among Harrogate's oldest hostelries, its extraordinary success since its twenty-first-century opening in the southern wing of the venerable White Hart Hotel guarantees its inclusion in any account of the modern town's most popular attractions. Given the demanding nature of today's clientele with regard to both food and drink, the Fat Badger's success would not be so constant if the provisions it serves were not consistently good. With the former, everything is supplied from the best sources, equal care being devoted to the ultimate presentation on customers' plates. But there are other factors contributing to the Fat Badger's success, as well as the all-important matter of its provisions, for no matter how fine these may be, their serving

The Fat Badger's delightful terrace. (Copyright HRH Group)

The Fat Badger's splendid bar. (Copyright HRH Group)

and consumption amidst dismal or commonplace surroundings would ensure failure. And here, the Fat Badger really comes into its own, both inside and outside its premises.

Called Harrogate's finest surviving building by Professor Sir Nikolaus Pevsner, the White Hart Hotel, that superb essay in early Victorian neoclassicism, stands proudly at the foot of Cold Bath Road, its great ashlar façade testifying to the high quality of architect G. T. Andrews' work. The southern end of the building has a delightful terrace, where – if one can no longer watch the great mail coaches roll into Harrogate behind a team of horses – scenes of great animation are evident to Fat Badger customers, from the activities of sportsmen on the Stray, pedestrians streaming up and down Cold Bath Road, and passing traffic. Inside, it is possible to imagine one's self back in the mail coach era, as the Badger's attractive interiors, with their wooden floors, intimate booths, the flickering glow of the handsome lamps, and the fine long timber bar, embellished with elaborate carving, all seem survivors of the great days of coaching. No wonder it is loved by visitors and regulars alike.

Festivals

Even after only a brief examination of Harrogate, most visitors will agree that the place is an ideal location for a festival, and during the early decades of the twentieth century several festivals were held in the town with great success. Perhaps the most celebrated were those music festivals held in 1927 and 1929, when such internationally famous composers as Bax, Elgar, Percy Grainger, Roger Quilter and Cyril Scott were participants. Then, in 1936, the creation of the Harrogate Competitive Music Festival began the continuing annual festival for young performing musicians, which – the war years apart – became an important and well-attended part of the town's cultural life.

After the Second World War, Sir John Barbirolli brought the Halle Orchestra to town in 1943, and this initial visit led to the annual visits when the orchestra stayed in Harrogate for six nights throughout the 1950s and 1960, making the Halle Music Festival an eagerly anticipated event. By the time 'glorious John' died in 1970, Harrogate had its own home-grown festival, the Harrogate International Festival of Arts and Sciences, which had been founded in 1966 by Clive Wilson. This is still with us today, although the fifty and more years since its creation have seen great changes in audience expectations, and economic conditions, all of which have meant that if Harrogate International Festivals were to survive, they had to adapt. Changes have included the launching in 1994 of the Spring Series of chamber music concerts, usually held at the Old Swan Hotel; the Theakston's Old Peculier Crime Writing Festival (a phenomenal success, and now the biggest in the world) founded in 2003; the Raworth Literary Festival, which started in 2012; the Harrogate History Festival of 2013; and the Berwins Salon North, set up in 2015. Truly, Harrogate had become a festival town *par excellence*.

Harrogate's festival season had taken on an international flavour in 1953 with the inauguration of French Week, which expanded in 1962 when an Italian Week was also introduced. National cultural events were arranged, exchange visits, and local

Theakston's Old Peculiar Crime Writing Festival in the magnificent Royal Hall. (Copyright Charlotte Graham Picture Shows, for Harrogate International Festivals)

The International Gilbert & Sullivan Festival – the National Gilbert & Sullivan Opera Company's production of *Pirates of Penzance*. (Copyright Jane Stokes, photographer)

shops mounted French- and Italian-themed displays, which imparted a Continental look to James and Parliament Streets, as well as Crescent Gardens. Even more of an international flavour came to town in 1973 with the first of the Harrogate International Youth Music Festivals, when concert bands from schools and colleges all over the world converged on Harrogate, giving the splendid young performers an international stage where they could not only display their native talent but also experience the skills of foreign youth. The annual parade through the town, often an Easter event, became a traffic-stopping delight, even if the weather was occasionally unkind.

In 2014, the world-famous International Gilbert and Sullivan Festival moved to Harrogate from Buxton, and at the time of writing is a highly successful part of the town's annual series of sparkling festivals, attracting visitors from all over the world. So in many respects, Harrogate deserves its 'Festival Town' status.

Fountain Court

Some of the author's happiest memories of his childhood in Harrogate are of family visits to the Fountain Court, that oasis of peace and tranquillity between Montpellier and Parliament Street, which from the time of its opening in 1939 by the Lord Mayor of London until its council-sponsored destruction in 2000 was a much-loved

F

refuge for residents and visitors alike, who, weary from site-seeing and shopping, sought refreshment and rest amidst traffic-free environs enhanced with hanging baskets, flower beds, a goldfish pool with fountain, and away from the view and noise and pollution of traffic. Bliss indeed!

The Fountain Court had been built along with the Lounge Hall and the so-called 'Western Wing Treatment Block' in 1938–9, as Harrogate's final attempt to maintain its lead over all other British Spas. The site for the new development to the south of the Royal Baths was filled with the Royal Baths' Wintergardens, a glazed promenade that some considered old-fashioned and draughty. Designed by Borough Surveyor

Above: The Fountain Court's Goldfish Pool *c.* 1965.

Right: An oasis of tranquility in the heart of the town.

The Fountain Court in summer.

Leonard Clark, who had also worked on the Market and the Sun Pavilion, the Fountain Court was the out-of-doors equivalent to the Lounge Hall, and was typical of the interwar's fashion for fresh air as an adjunct to health. The square Fountain Court was open to the sky but surrounded with a superb colonnade in the Tuscan order, which held aloft a glazed ceiling that ran around all four sides of the forum. Visitors therefore had the choice of sitting in fresh air under cover or in the open. The centre of the court had a pool filled with goldfish and a fountain, the soothing tinkle of which provided a backdrop to the conversations of visitors. On hot days, the tables were provided with sun umbrellas, and during music recitals in the adjoining Lounge Hall, the connecting doors were thrown wide open so that the music of the piano trio could waft over those sitting outside.

For some, the Fountain Court seemed to enshrine the spirit of Harrogate, and over eighty years on, what a crowd-drawing asset the Fountain Court would be. But alas, in less civilised times, and with a council in power for whom the Royal Baths were seen as a problem to be rid of rather than an asset to be cultivated, the Fountain Court was an impediment to the newly planned car park, so it was demolished to provide space for *nine cars.* How very foolish.

Friends

It is surely a sign of the pleasantness of Harrogate as a place to live that it has seen the growth of so many organisations of Friends. Friends of Harrogate District Hospital and Community Charity, who do such wonderful work in fundraising; Friends of Harrogate Theatre; Friends of the District's Museums; Friends of the Mercer Art Gallery; Friends of Harrogate International Festivals; Friends of this, that, and nearly everything else, all providing a means for well-meaning volunteers to devote their time and energy to good causes. There are the Friends of the Library, who try to do as volunteers what chartered librarians such as the author spent years at university learning how to do for a livelihood; there are the original friends, the Society of Friends, usually known as 'Quakers', who seem to have first appeared in Harrogate in 1656; and there are the Friends of the Royal Hall, in reality the Trustees, whose tireless campaigning and fundraising from 2001 to 2008 ensured the magnificent monument was saved, and who continue to the present to work for its embellishment. As these words are being written, another Friends group has been formed, the 'Friends of Harrogate Town Centre', whose purpose is to 'bring back the sparkle to the town centre'. All these Friends contribute tirelessly to the town's welfare, and all deserve our thanks – some, perhaps, more than others.

The Friends of Harrogate, no longer active, were the oldest of the town's organised Friends apart from the Quakers. They were set up in 1946 as part of the spirit of revival

The Friends of Harrogate *c.* 1972, with Lady Bomanji (seated).

that permeated the country after the Second World War. They had been the idea of the mayor, Councillor J. S. Tennant, who felt the town could use an organisation of people committed to the advancement of Harrogate: 'I think it vital that the Friends should be as broadly based as possible; the last thing we want is that they should be small and select...they should be open to all who had the welfare of Harrogate at heart.' In their early days, the Friends promoted the welfare of Harrogate in general, as well as research into the medicinal advantages of spa therapy, and they encouraged improvements to the town's horticultural and arboricultural amenities, also arranging lectures and visits to places of interest.

One of the most high-profiled groups of Friends in Harrogate is the Friends of Valley Gardens, which has had a two-part life. The Friends of Valley Gardens came into being in 1986 to prevent the construction of a car park within the gardens and also to encourage the restoration of the badly neglected Sun Pavilion. Chairman Mrs Anne Smith, with the active support of TV gardener Geoffrey Smith (no relation) and world-famous author James Herriot, roused public opinion so greatly that the car park was thrown out, and – after a prolonged campaign – the restored Sun Pavilion was reopened by Her Majesty the Queen on 10 December 1998. Twenty years later,

Anne Smith and Geoffrey Smith (no relation). (Copyright Mrs A. Smith)

Jane Blayney (gold jacket) and Friends of Valley Gardens with Mayor Nigel Sims at the opening of the restored Old Magnesia Well Pump Room. (Copyright *Harrogate Advertiser*)

and in different circumstances, the Friends of Valley Gardens (with the help of Tom Holleman) succeeded in establishing a lively volunteer group, who – working in collaboration with Harrogate Borough Council's own staff – contribute valuable input to the maintenance of the much-loved gardens. Three outstanding achievements of recent years have been the 2015 restoration of the lovely little Gothic Magnesia Well Pump Room of 1858, which is now used as a centre of information about Valley Gardens; the installation in 2018 of the impressive Edward VII Peace Gate in Valley Drive; and the refurbishment of the badly neglected Japanese Garden, also in 2018, which in a memorable ceremony was opened by the Japanese Ambassador. The chairman of the Friends of Valley Gardens during the initiation and progress of these last three achievements was Mrs Jane Blayney, and it is certainly true that without the work of Jane Blayney, her distinguished predecessor Anne Smith and all of the wonderful volunteers who worked with them, visitors to today's Valley Gardens would be faced by a very different, and less attractive, prospect.

Grand Duchess George of Russia

Marie Georgievna, born on 3 March 1876, was the fifth child of King George I and Queen Olga of Greece, and a member of the royal house of Schleswig-Holstein-Sonderburg-Glucksburg. She married Grand Duke George Mikhailovich of Russia in 1900, thus becoming a member of the Imperial Russian family. The Grand Duchess's two daughters, Nina, born in 1901, and Xenia, born in 1903, had delicate health, partly the result of the often extreme climatic conditions of their homeland, and when this came to the attention of the Russian Empress Alexandra Feodorovna, who had benefited greatly from her visit to Harrogate in 1894, she recommended that Grand Duchess George should take her children to the Yorkshire spa where their health would improve.

Grand Duchess George first brought her daughters to Harrogate in July 1910 where they had treatment at the Royal Baths and participated in Harrogate's glittering social 'season', their health benefiting in consequence. This so impressed the Grand Duchess that she repeated the visit every summer, the family becoming familiar faces at Harrogate. In the summer of 1914, Grand Duchess George brought her two daughters to Harrogate for their annual visit, and returned to London as a guest of King George, her intention being to eventually travel back to Russia with her daughters and her aunt, the Dowager Russian Empress, who was visiting her sister, Queen Alexandra. When war was imminent, the Grand Duchess had to retrieve her daughters from Harrogate, where she arrived at midday on 4 August, but by then war had been declared. Almost immediately, and realising – as did very few – that the war would be on an unprecedented scale with massive casualties, the Grand Duchess opened a hospital for wounded servicemen, which was so successful that further establishments were opened, including a convalescent home. By the time the war ended in 1918, the Grand Duchess' Harrogate hospitals had dealt with many severely wounded men, only nine of whom died of their wounds. It must not be thought that the Grand Duchess and her colleagues, many of whom were themselves royalty, did not participate in the day-to-day running of the hospitals. After training, they all became Red Cross nurses, and performed the most basic and menial tasks in the wards, including helping the surgeons during operations and nursing the men as they recovered.

Above left: Grand Duchess George and Princesses Xenia and Nina.

Above right: Tewit Well Hospital in 1914.

    After the war, which saw Grand Duke George murdered by the Bolsheviks, the Grand Duchess eventually remarried and settled in Rome until her pro-British attitude attracted the unwelcome attention of Mussolini's secret police, whose persecutions caused her to flee to Greece, where she died on 14 December 1940, only weeks before Hitler's invasion.

Harrogate Spring Water

Harrogate's spring water is one of the biggest success stories in the history of the town. Since 1999, when plans were announced for a private company to relaunch Harrogate's most celebrated product, the international demand for bottled Harrogate Water has exceeded original expectations so greatly that the discreetly designed and beautifully landscaped bottling plant on Harlow Moor Road, built on land specifically acquired by Harrogate Borough Council in 1923–4 as an adjunct to its Water Undertaking, has had to increase its capacity several times. It is difficult to avoid superlatives when describing this phenomenal product, which is not a strong-tasting mineral water, dominated by one particular mineral such as sulphur or iron, but a remarkably pure and perfectly balanced natural source water that flows from the great sandstone dome beneath Harlow Moor. Even in the hottest, driest summers, it never ceases to flow.

When the first bottles of this Harrogate Water appeared in 2002, the Harrogate Spa Water Ltd company witnessed a phenomenal success for their product, which within only a year won prizes such as the internationally celebrated Berkeley Springs International Water Tasting Award for the world's best carbonated bottled water. That same year also saw Harrogate Water being chosen by Buckingham Palace to supply

Harrogate Spring Water Plant. (Copyright Harrogate Spring Water)

The Harrogate Spring Water team. (Copyright Harrogate Spring Water)

the Queen's dances. Since then, the rise and rise of this wonderful natural product has been dizzying, and by 2013, Managing Director James Cain was reporting an enviable annual growth rate of over 30 per cent. This was why in 2013 the plant received a 23,000-square foot extension to the state-of-the-art main plant, and a further 5,500-square meter extension in 2018, where recyclable bottles are manufactured to the most exacting environmental requirements. The bottles are particularly eye-catching, all being recyclable, and have won several highly prestigious awards; the firm is also proud of its partnership with 'Keep Britain Tidy'.

Today, Harrogate Water is found all over the world, including top catering businesses and airlines, and has become a favourite with many celebrities. In April 2019 Harrogate Spring Water began a contract with British Airways, which joined such other customers as Royal Ascot and the Royal Albert Hall, all of which show that the vision of its promoters back in 2000 has been amply rewarded, and has literally taken the name of Harrogate flying around the world, as well as providing a much-needed boost to the town's economy. But above all, it is delicious to consume, being *the perfect* naturally sourced water – still or sparkling.

Still and Sparkling. (Copyright Harrogate Spring Water)

Italian Week

Both French and Italian Weeks were once such an important part of the Harrogate year that they should be considered as two aspects of the same thing, i.e. the need to foster international goodwill by encouraging the study of foreign languages and exchange visits. The original conception came from His Majesty's Consul General in Strasbourg, who, in a letter dated 15 December 1949 to Harrogate's Town Clerk, suggested that the town should stimulate a close relationship with the French resort of Colmar, in Alsace. Harrogate's town council, prompted no doubt by memories of the recent war, embraced the concept with enthusiasm, the outcome being that the

French Week in Crescent Gardens *c.* 1958.

The beginning
of Italian Week
in 1963.

resort of Luchon, rather than Colmar, became twinned with Harrogate. The First French Week occurred in May 1953, when members of the French government visited Harrogate, along with the Luchon mayor, Monsieur Alfred Coste-Floret, and his party. Special programmes on French themes were provided in the town's galleries, museums, cinemas, public halls, hotels and shops, and the whole thing was such a huge success that it not only became a much-anticipated public event, but it was also followed in 1962 by the council's decision to twin with the Italian spa resort of Montecatini, whose mayor, Signor Bruno Barni, in company with the Italian Ambassador, were welcomed to Harrogate's historic Council Chamber by Mayor Norman Morrell.

Much of the credit for the success of the town-twinning movement in Harrogate must go to the wholehearted enthusiasm of the council, which understood that adequate financing was essential; to such council officers as Entertainments Manager Bill Baxter (himself an accomplished linguist), who organised wonderful programmes of events; and to the general public, who relished the whole experience, from the comic waiters races held in Parliament Street and Crescent Gardens, to the Italian or French music recitals in the Royal Hall and the Continental-themed shop window displays throughout the town.

A waiters'
race during
Italian Week.

J

Jespers

Jespers, the celebrated stationer of Oxford Street, is an old Harrogate institution, long famed for its high standards of service and the high quality of its products. Foster Barritt Jesper established an engraver's business in 1901 at Prospect Crescent, Harrogate, which was continued in the 1930s by his son Denis Mellor Jesper, both men being master engravers, F. B. Jesper having engraved jewellery for Princess

Jespers window during the Tour de Yorkshire. (Copyright Jespers)

Mary and many London Jewellers too. At the outbreak of war in 1939 Denis and his foreman Jack Elsworth received their call-up papers, but following a confidential visit from the Admiralty, these were withdrawn and they were asked to undertake top-secret work on the government's radar project, which involved engraving panels for installations. Within a decade of the war's ending, Denis's son Charles introduced business stationery, typewriters and office furniture to the business, which then had premises in Parliament Terrace. Denis and Charles seized the opportunity to develop the family firm further by taking a larger shop at No. 27 Oxford Street. The firm subsequently moved to its current location at No. 14 in 1966 when Marks and Spencer acquired the land between Cambridge Street and Oxford Street (including the former St Peter's vicarage) to expand their store.

Although demand for engraving services was in decline, Harrogate Borough Council's seventy-fifth anniversary in 1959 saw Jespers engraving much of the civic silver presented to the town by well-wishers. In the late 1960s a move to No. 14 saw Jespers really flourish as a specialist retail stationer, becoming agents for many famous brands in the fine writing instrument and stationery world and culminating in Jespers being awarded UK retail stationer of the year in 1989.

Interior of Jespers. (Copyright Jespers)

Following the deaths of Foster B. Jesper in 1965 and Denis M. Jesper in 1978, Charles Jesper took over the business, and this store has welcomed many famous faces including James Herriot (Jespers sold this famous author his typewriters and word-processors), Chris Bonington, Diana Rigg, Dustin Hofmann, Vanessa Redgrave, Robin Day, Michael Barrymore and Shirley Williams. Today, Charles' son Peter is the fourth generation of the Jesper family to lead the business and is the current managing director. In 2019, following the retirement of the Jesper family, the business was acquired by Vickers & Morris.

Johnston, Sergeant Major Robert

The monument to Sergeant Major Robert Johnston must surely be regarded as one of the most interesting in Grove Road Cemetery, as it commemorates the life and achievement of one of the King's Royal Irish Hussars, who on 25 October 1854 participated in the suicidal 'charge of the Light Brigade' during the war in Crimea. The remarkable fact about Sergeant Major Johnston's part in the infamous charge was not so much that he participated, but that he lived through it, one of only 195 men out of 600 to survive the brutal Russian cannon fire. The monument also records his service at Alma, Balaclava, Inkerman, Tchernaya, Bulancak, McKenzie's

Sergeant Major Johnston's monument at Grove Road cemetery.

Farm, Kertch, Yeni-kale, Kotah, Chudaree, and seven battles. Sergeant Major Johnston died in Harrogate Infirmary on 28 November 1882, and his monument records only that it was 'erected by a friend'. One hundred and thirty years later, the monument was restored, thanks to the selfless respect of four Harrogate ex-servicemen – Peter Burrell, his brother Thomas, John Leng, and Jim McDonald – who determined to discover as much as they could about Sergeant Major Johnston's life. They could not find where he was born, where he lived before he came to Harrogate, nor could any likeness be found. However, it was discovered that Sergeant Major Johnston had been employed by the Liverpool-based firm of William Gossage. It is probable, given the number of his military engagements, that the sergeant major came to Harrogate to recover his health, as the Yorkshire spa was then nationally celebrated as a place for recuperation.

It is known that he entered the Cottage Hospital in Tower Street, which still stands on the junction with Belford Road, where he died on 28 November 1882, aged forty-nine. The funeral was very well attended, with crowds lining the streets to watch the cortege arriving at St Peter's Church, with a sword and carbine placed on the coffin. By the time the cortege reached Grove Road, crowds had to be cleared before the funeral could proceed. It was said that the crowd numbered 20,000, and this at a time when the population of Harrogate was only 12,000.

In 1984 efforts were made to restore the monument. The sum of £1,000 was raised. In addition, the four men responsible raised a further £100, which enabled a plaque to be placed in St Peter's Church, following an exhibition in St Luke's Church rooms, attended by Mayor Brenda Towler. It would not surprise the author to learn that in another 130 years, there will be those who will again step forward to secure the future of Sergeant Major Johnston's name.

Kissingen

At one time, the Kissingen Well was one of Harrogate's most celebrated mineral waters, being of the family known as saline iron, which were themselves of the Chalybeate class. The Kissingen water was discovered in 1833 when the laying of the foundations for the Crown, or Montpellier Baths, led to it being found near to the Crescent Road boundary of the Crown Hotel's gardens. When analysis showed that the water had qualities similar to the Rigozzi Well at the famous German spa of Bad Kissingen, the newly discovered Harrogate water was named the 'Kissingen Well'. This may have been done as an attempt to encourage British travellers who were contemplating a visit to the German spa to visit Harrogate instead, where the same type of mineral waters could be had. According to such analysts as West, Hofmann, and Muspratt, the Kissingen waters were particularly rich in chloride of sodium, carbonate of barium, chloride of calcium, chloride of magnesium, carbonate of iron and silica, the total of grains per gallon being 874.740. However, when Arnold Woodmansey analysed

Borough Analyst
Arnold Woodmansey
c. 1940.

The Grand Pump Room at the Royal Baths.

the Kissingen water in the mid-twentieth century, he found that it was the result of merging at least two separate springs, which, moreover, varied in their mineral constituency. This made analysis a very unreliable process, as the waters' mineral components could change on an almost daily process. Yet despite this, the Kissingen became one of Harrogate's most popular waters, especially after it was aerated and bottled. The final entry in the Corporation's order book before the council closed down their water-bottling business was dated 19 March 1947, for one dozen 24-ounce bottles of Kissingen water at fifteen shillings, plus nine shillings and six pence postage and packing, ordered by a Mr J. H. Wright of North Street, Beeston, Nottinghamshire. This author recalls that the Kissingen water was dispensed from the Royal Bath's Grand Pump Room until 1969, when Harrogate Borough Council chose to end nearly 400 years of dispensing the amazing waters given to it by a provident nature.

Kursaal

The Kursaal, or Cure-Hall, is the German term for buildings erected in connection with a spa undertaking that included provision for entertainment. German spas were highly fashionable towards the end of the nineteenth century, when many of the names and terms used in German spas were copied by their foreign rivals. Harrogate, for example had its Nauheim Bath, its Schwalbach Bath and its Gobel equipment, and when in 1898 the town began to consider the provision of a larger entertainment facility than the Royal Spa Rooms of 1835, it naturally adopted the fashionable German name of Kursaal. For centuries, the medical profession had recognised the importance of entertainment as a means of relieving stress, and spas developed the habit of not only providing pump rooms and baths where the physical aspects of the spa 'cure' could be had, but also of providing theatres, concert and music halls where the mental aspects of the cure could also be satisfied – thus the term 'Cure-Hall' or to use the German equivalent, 'Kursaal'.

Harrogate's Kursaal was the result of a competition of 1899 that was won by architect Robert Beale, whose design was chosen by the Corporation's assessor, Frank Matcham, who was the greatest theatrical designer of his age. In an inspired moment, the Corporation asked Matcham to work with Beale to develop his original entry, the result of which opened in 1903 to widespread acclaim, one description of which

The Royal Hall's gorgeous interior. (Copyright Harrogate Convention Centre)

was 'a palace of glittering gold'. The Kursaal had a seating capacity for around 1,300, its main auditorium being surrounded with an ambulatory where guests could exercise their bodies by walking around its 360-degree perimeter. Another unique feature was that the main hall's floor was flat, to enable the rows of seats to be removed for such events as balls, fashion shows, civic events or political rallies. It was this flexibility of use that ensured the much-loved building would survive into the post-spa age.

The greatest artists of the day appeared on the Kursaal's stage, and rather than listing them, it is easier to observe that the only missing name is that of Caruso, who was supposed to appear in October 1914, but the outbreak of war in August 1914 led to his engagement being cancelled. In 1918, the council changed the name of the Kursaal to that of the Royal Hall, and throughout the 1920s and 1930, the screening of films became an important part of the building's programmes. Much of Matcham's wonderful scheme of decoration was lost in the late 1920s, when a simpler scheme of painting was introduced, but following the crisis of 2001–06, when structural problems nearly led to the Royal Hall being demolished, a programme of restoration from 2006–08 resurrected its original magnificent appearance. When HRH The Prince of Wales reopened the restored Royal Hall on 22 January 2008, Harrogate had its finest interior back in public use.

The Royal Hall at night. (Copyright Harrogate Convention Centre)

L

Lupton, Betty

Elizabeth Lupton, generally known as Betty, was regarded for decades as the symbol of Harrogate. Her honorary title of 'Queen of the Well' indicated that she was regarded as the most senior of the several 'well women' who served the visitors who frequented the famous Old Sulphur Well that now flows beneath the Royal Pump Room.

The Royal Pump Room of 1842 with its 1913 annex.

Her date of birth is unknown, but was probably in *c.* 1759 or 1760. Her life was traced by Harrogate historian H. H. Walker, who discovered that she had died on 15 August 1843 in the home of her daughter, Mrs Downham, at No. 7 Prospect Place. Before this, Betty had lived in Diamond Cottage, No. 6 Kensington Square, where between 1837 and 1840 she occasionally took in up to two guests. Although she worked as an unpaid attendant at the wells, primarily the Old Sulphur Well, the visitors' sometimes generous tips provided a living income. There are several surviving accounts of Betty having a sharp tongue, particularly if a visitor was sufficiently unwise to doubt the efficacy of the Sulphur Water as a cure.

When the Harrogate Improvement Commissioners built the Royal Pump Room in 1842, the well women were able to work in more pleasant conditions, and in recognition of Betty's outstanding service as 'a very old attendant at the well', the Improvement Commissioners resolved on 7 August 1843 to pay her seven shillings a week. Alas, old Betty, who was still working at the age of around eighty-four, enjoyed her new wage for only eight days before her death. Although there are no photographs of old Betty, the silhouette reproduced opposite was generally regarded as a good likeness, and Harrogate Museum still maintains the table and water ladle used by her throughout her long career.

Above left: Betty Lupton's house at No. 6 Kensington Square in 1953.

Above right: Silhouette of Betty Lupton.

Mayoralty

Robert Ackrill had the honour of being Harrogate's first mayor, as it was he who, in 1884, was appointed Charter Mayor by the Charter of Incorporation signed by Queen Victoria that made Harrogate a fully incorporated borough. For such newly created authorities as Harrogate, it was the Charter Mayor's responsibility to oversee the revision of the burgess lists and to make them open for public inspection. He also had to oversee the subsequent elections for councillors, aldermen, etc., and to ensure that the conditions of Incorporation contained in the charter were fulfilled. But in the generally understood meaning of the office, it was Nicholas Carter who was chosen by his colleagues (formerly Improvement Commissioners, but after the elections, fully fledged councillors) to be Harrogate's first elected mayor. Since Nicholas Carter first donned the mayoral robes and chain of office, there have been well over 125 men and women to serve the town, not only by presiding over meetings of the elected councillors, but perhaps more importantly acting as its first citizen

Nicholas Carter, Harrogate's first mayor.

to be the representative of every one of the town's residents, regardless of class or party. The most honourable of Harrogate's mayors have always placed the interests of the community above party politics, and have tried to ensure that the interests of powerful pressure groups do not silence the interests of the minority voice.

Since 1884, such councillors as Richard Ellis, George Dawson, Charles Fortune, Samson Fox, and David Simpson worked during the Victorian Age to bring Harrogate to the peak of its perfection, providing inspiration to their successors in the mayoral role. After the election of Mary Fisher as mayor in 1949, women were at last able to contribute to the office of mayor, and when in 1957 Queen Elizabeth made her first visit to Harrogate as monarch, it was the town's second female mayor, Alice Wardle, who greeted Her Majesty at Harrogate railway station.

For any visitor to the town, be they holiday maker, tourist, conference attender or exhibitor, a meeting with the mayor represents the ultimate civic honour, as the mayor is the very symbol of Harrogate, and represents every one of the community's citizens. The mayor is also the monarch's representative. None of this could be transferred successfully to a paid official or political figure, because the mystique of over 136 years that has grown around the role of the mayor of Harrogate belongs to this office alone. Yet despite the unquestioned success of the mayoral office, and the wonderful contributions of so many publicly minded citizens in carrying out this role, voices are occasionally heard calling for the mayoralty to be abolished. This author has no doubts that such a move would be retrograde. Those who may promote abolition may themselves be without an understanding of the significance of history for the people, or its role as a visitor attraction, but this is no reason to inflict such a view upon the community. The people of Harrogate should fight to retain their mayoralty, which is within the reach of every citizen of voting age.

Queen Elizabeth at Harrogate railway station with Mayor Alice Wardle, 10 July 1957.

Above: Mayor and Mayoress Nick and Linda Brown in the Crescent Gardens Mayoral Parlour. (Copyright Councillor Nick Brown)

Below: The Mayor and Mayoress with Mayoral Chaplain Clive Handford and MP Andrew Jones. (Copyright Councillor Nick Brown)

New Zealand

On 21 June 1954, the deputy mayor of Wellington, New Zealand, Councillor E. R. Topp, opened the New Zealand Garden in Harrogate's Valley Gardens, in the presence of the mayor of Harrogate, Councillor Don Christelow. The New Zealand Garden was the result of a visit made to Wellington early in 1953 by Sir Bernard Lomas Walker, the man responsible for the daring move to plant crocus bulbs on the Stray after the Second World War. This was at a time when most of the councillors had experience of the war, and retained strong feelings of kinship for allies such as New Zealand, who had contributed so much in the struggle, with twenty-three New Zealand airmen stationed in the locality, having lost their lives in the conflict. Consequently, Harrogate Council planned a memorial garden, and decided to present the city of Wellington with a replica of Harrogate's own mace, made by Ogden's of James Street, which was handed over by Sir Bernard Lomas Walker. In return, the city of Wellington presented Harrogate with a fine painting by Marcus White of the city of Wellington seen from the Tinakori Hills. The man in charge of the new garden's formation was Mr W. V. Bishop, Harrogate's parks and gardens supervisor, who perhaps more than anyone else was responsible for the transformation of the town that occurred after the end of the Second World War. The location was a little-used corner of Valley Gardens between the public conveniences, and Cornwall Road. Plants for the New Zealand Garden were grown in New Zealand and shipped over to England on the *Dominium Monarch*, which arrived in Southampton in March 1953. Seeds had also been despatched from New Zealand, which arrived at the Harlow Hill nurseries from Christchurch, New Zealand. The *Harrogate Advertiser* noted at the time that the plants were the only known collection of New Zealand plants outside Kew, and that the name tags were in both Maori and Latin. To complete the garden, a flagpole was provided that flew the New Zealand flag, thus ensuring that Harrogate's New Zealand connection was clearly displayed. When the mayor of Wellington, Frank Kitts, visited Harrogate in June 1960, the mayor of Harrogate was Councillor L. Roberts. By this time the New Zealand Garden had matured, and shows the mayors of Wellington and of Harrogate visiting the New Zealand Garden in company with Mr Bishop, and Mr T. J. Hunt OBE, of the central office of Information. Mr Bishop may be seen at the far right.

Above: The mayors of Wellington, New Zealand and Harrogate in the New Zealand Gardens in 1960.

Below: The newly restored New Zealand Garden in 2010. (Copyright Jane Blayney)

The New Zealand Garden became somewhat neglected during subsequent decades, but was beautifully restored in 2010, with a ceremony of rededication on 12 August, when the mayor of Harrogate, Councillor Bill Hoult, warmly welcomed guests who included a party from New Zealand with Councillor Ray Ahipene-Mercer, who had the title of Elder (Kaumatua); Sam Poutu Jackson (Elder); and Mrs June Te Raumanga Jackson from Wellington City. The New Zealand Garden has also been embellished with some rather wonderful sculptures on traditional Maori subjects.

Nidd Gorge at Bilton

Today, there must be few in either Harrogate or Knaresborough who know that for centuries the medieval boundary between the two communities was that of the River Nidd. This changed when the Great Award of 1778 became effective, when Harrogate lost huge swathes of its former territory to Knaresborough. The long-term advantage of this arrangement was that nineteenth- and twentieth-century Harrogate's extensive urbanisation left the banks of the River Nidd largely untouched, something that the building of Bilton Mill, before 1303, and Scotton Flax Mill,

Bilton Viaduct, Nidd Gorge. (Copyright Bilton Conservation Group)

in 1798, hardly affected. Significant change occurred when the operation of the Leeds Northern Railway line between Starbeck and Ripley, Pateley Bridge, Ripon and Thirsk entailed the building of a large stone viaduct across the River Nidd. Standing 104 feet above the river, this imposing, seven-arched monument to the railway age was built in 1848, and last carried railway traffic in 1967. Today it carries walkers, as well as the delightful Sustrans cycle path, and is situated amidst the beautiful and highly valued ecosystem that is Nidd Gorge.

Some fifteen years after railway traffic ceased passing over the viaduct, Harrogate Borough Council established the Nidd Gorge Management Trust, who were charged with making the area more accessible to hikers and cyclists. The old riverside path became dangerous after heavy rain, but the placing of Duck Boards at strategic locations ensured that the path could continue to be used. Much of the flanking woodland, which has become beautiful thanks to careful managing, is cared for by the Woodland Trust, and throughout the year, visitors can enjoy a lovely variety of plant life. This in turn has become home to wildlife, and Nidd Gorge is celebrated as home to several species of ladybirds, butterflies and birds preferring a mixture of deciduous and coniferous woodland. Altogether, a delight, and certainly one of Harrogate's assets.

Garlic Walk, Bilton Gorge. (Copyright Bilton Conservation Group)

O

Ogden

'Welcome to Bond Street on the moors!' read the banner draped across James Street in 1913 to welcome the Lord Mayor of London as he drove in state to the opening of the Royal Pump Room's annex. And for many of Harrogate's fashionable visitors, James Street as a retail area did indeed enshrine the essence of Bond Street, with its exclusive fashion shops, wine merchants and jewellers, of which the business established in 1893 by James Roberts Ogden was at the head. Over a century and a quarter later, the Ogden business can be said to have not only survived, but survived and flourished, thanks to two things: unsurpassed quality of stock, and service dedicated to the total satisfaction of customers – things perhaps obvious enough to name, but very difficult

Ogden's James Street premises. (Copyright Ogden's)

to achieve, and even more difficult to maintain for over 125 years. Over this time, the firm has served members of the royal family, American presidents, and other key public figures such as King George VI and Winston Churchill. Now run by the fifth generation of the founder's family, Ogden's handsome premises at No. 38 James Street still lie at the heart of Harrogate's shopping quarter.

Today, the business stocks the world's greatest brands of watches, including Zenith and Longines, as well as items from Fope, an Italian gold jewellery manufacturer established in 1929, and Georg Jensen, founded in Copenhagen in 1904 to manufacture high-quality tableware, watches and jewellery. Expert craftsmen maintain the firm's high standards, their workshop being on the premises rather than some distance away. In 2014 this workshop was fitted with a glass wall so that clients could witness work at first-hand. One of the first-floor displays tells the story of this family firm and its employees through old documents and photographs; those dating from the time of the First World War and also those relating to J. R. Ogden's work as an expert archaeologist are both moving and revealing.

Ogden's specialist repair workshop. (Copyright Ogden's)

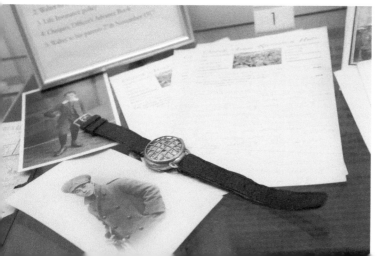

A poignant display in the Ogden museum. (Copyright Ogden's)

P

Pinewoods

Enter these enchanted woods,
You who dare

Despite their name, the Pinewoods do not consist solely of pine trees. During the nineteenth and early twentieth centuries, many European spas planted pine trees around their perimeters to ensure that as the wind blew, it wafted the scent of pine

The Pinewoods, Harlow Moor. (Courtesy of Neil Hind, Pinewoods Conservation Group)

across the urban area, thus improving the quality of the air. What was done by other spas had naturally to be done in Harrogate, which had long prided itself on being ahead of all other spa resorts, but here, the ideal location to the immediate west of the Old Sulphur Well was not in the town's hands, but since the Great Award of 1778 was held by the Earls of Harewood. In 1893 Harrogate Corporation began to lease land on Harlow Moor from Lord Harewood, which the earl agreed to sell in 1898 for £30,500. This land lay on the hillside to the west of Bogs Field, continuing as far west as what became Harlow Moor Road, and thus greatly extended the size of Valley Gardens and Bogs Field. The planting that followed included pine trees, but their number was considerably increased after 1924 when the Corporation acquired a further 65 acres

Maintaining the woodland. (Courtesy of Neil Hind, Pinewoods Conservation Group)

of land from Lord Harewood, which lay to the immediate west of Harlow Moor Road as far as Crag Lane. It was this land that was then planted with many pine trees, which gave their name to the entire woodland area. Ostensibly, Harrogate Corporation acquired the Pinewoods to enhance the recreational significance of the area, and to maintain its role in protecting the mineral wells of Bogs Field and Low Harrogate from building, which might affect adversely the geological strata through which the mineral waters flowed. Today, the Pinewoods encompasses a little over 96 acres of gorgeous woodland.

In October 2002 a number of public-spirited volunteers formed the Pinewoods Conservation Group, which not only promoted the maintenance and conservation of the environment within the Harrogate area and especially the Pinewoods, but also oppose moves to degrade and diminish this wonderful public amenity. Working in co-operation with Harrogate Borough Council, the Pinewoods Conservation Group – a registered charity since January 2003 – assists the conservation of the natural habitat of the area's wildlife, and advances the education of the public in the use of woodlands by encouraging them to participate in the management of the woods.

The Pinewoods Conservation Group at work. (Courtesy of Neil Hind, Pinewoods Conservation Group)

Queen Elizabeth II

Queen Elizabeth's first Harrogate visit occurred on Wednesday 27 July 1949, when some four years before her coronation, Princess Elizabeth arrived in Harrogate with the Duke of Edinburgh to attend the Great Yorkshire Show. The mayor at this time was Councillor Mary Fisher, the first woman to hold the office, and the Hotel Majestic's banquet to celebrate the princess's arrival included the Lord Lieutenant of the West Riding of Yorkshire. The image opposite shows Princess Elizabeth outside the Hotel Majestic.

Princess Elizabeth at the Majestic in 1949.

Queen Elizabeth at the Harrogate Convention Centre. (Copyright Harrogate Convention Centre)

Harrogate has been in royal hands since 1399, when at Henry IV's coronation he declared that henceforth, the Duchy of Lancaster would always be the monarch's property. This was reduced in time, particularly by Charles I and George III, the last of whom sold large parts of the royal forest – of which Harrogate was a part – whilst retaining the most valuable portions in Harrogate. To this day, the subsoil of Harrogate's most famous attribute, the 200 acres of the Stray, is owned by the monarch, which places Harrogate firmly among the most royal of boroughs.

Queen Elizabeth made her second official visit to Harrogate in April 1985, when she was greeted at Harrogate railway station by Mayor Alec MacCarroll, where she visited the new Conference Centre before continuing to Ripon for the royal Maundy service. A further royal visit occurred in December 1998, when Her Majesty opened the newly restored Sun Pavilion, and also visited Harrogate Theatre and the home of Farrah's Harrogate Toffee.

Queen Victoria

To commemorate Queen Victoria's Golden Jubilee in 1887, Richard Ellis presented his home town with a statue of Queen Victoria, and the land on which it was built, located in Station Square at the top of James Street. The Golden Jubilee Monument took the form of a square Gothic plinth, surmounted with a canopied spire, beneath which was placed a standing statue of Queen Victoria, sculpted by Webber in Thomas Holroyd's

Esplanade studio. Designed by Arthur Bown, the gorgeous little monument remains a perfect example of High Victorian public art, although the unnecessary removal in 1941 of the surrounding ornamental railings with their gas lamps diminished its appearance. The foundation stone was laid by Mrs Ellis on 14 April 1887, and the monument was officially presented to the town on 23 June 1887. The completed Victoria monument was unveiled by the Marquis of Ripon on 6 October 1888, with the statue of the queen gazing towards the site of the unbuilt Town Hall, where ever since it has seemed to enshrine the very spirit of Harrogate.

As to the often-asked question, did Victoria ever visit Harrogate? The usual answer is 'no!' apart from the occasion at 2.00 p.m. on 7 September 1858 when on her way to open Leeds' magnificent new Town Hall, the queen's royal train passed through Starbeck railway station. However, it was during a meeting at the Brunswick (later Prince of Wales) Hotel on 30 December 1861 that the architect of the Royal Pump Room, the unimpeachably reliable Isaac Thomas Shutt, in a discussion about the late Betty Lupton, stated the following words: 'Her Majesty herself when about fifteen or so, if I remember rightly, took the water (i.e., the water of the Old Sulphur Well) at her hands when she drove over from Harewood, and everybody swallowed and believed everything which old Betty gave and said.' This statement, had others not known it to have been true, would certainly have been disputed or contradicted either during that meeting or at later ones, but this never occurred. So, if one accepts Isaac Thomas Shutt's words, then Victoria *did* visit Harrogate, although she had not then been crowned as queen. It would be nice if one day, some generous and patriotic soul were to restore the monument's decorative lamps and railings.

Below left: Queen Victoria monument with railings *c.* 1902.

Below right: Queen Victoria monument in Station Square.

R

RHS Trial Gardens, Harlow Carr

RHS stands for Royal Horticultural Society, who since 2001 have administered the wonderful gardens established in 1949 by the Northern Horticultural Society at Harlow Carr's Crag Lane. The gardens were introduced as a northern counterpart to the south of England's RHS at Wisley, for 'promoting and developing the science, art and practice of horticulture, with special reference to the conditions pertaining to the north of England'. The new society had tried to establish itself in Harrogate in 1926, when it identified Harlow Moor as an ideal site for the trial gardens they wished to establish for the particular purpose of assessing the suitability of plants for northern climes, but had to wait for over twenty years before achieving this. At 500 feet, or 150 meters above sea level, with an acid soil (varying between pH.4.8 and pH.5.6), and exposed to the north-west winds that blew in from the nearby moors, the site of a wooded valley was not without its challenges, but these added to, rather than detracted from, the setting. It was particularly fortunate for the future development

Main borders at Harlow Carr in 1951.

of the RHS Gardens at Harlow Carr that in 1954 Geoffrey Smith (1928–2009) was appointed as superintendent. One of the twentieth century's great British gardeners, Geoffrey Smith's lifetime services were recognised in 1972 when he was made an Associate of Honour to the Royal Horticultural Society, and in 1988 when he received an honorary master's degree from the Open University. A regular media contributor, Geoffrey Smith's greatest achievement may still be seen at the gardens of the RHS at Harlow Carr, where he remained at the helm until his retirement in 1974.

Regular visits to these wonderful gardens reveal a constantly changing landscape. The work of nature and the life cycle of the plants, shrubs and trees with their seasonal diversity ensures that with even weekly visits there is always something fresh to discover. The work of man also ensures regular change, as new methods of planting are tried, further expanses of land incorporated, new buildings given an old use or old buildings provided with something new. Thanks to the Bramall Learning Centre, schoolchildren, botanists and RHS members now have a first-rate educational resource available, near the pleasant café and restaurant. The size of the gardens, and the truly astonishing variety of things to see within their bounds, means that visitors should allow at least a full half-day for their visit. At the time of writing, the gardens have announced exciting plans for the reintegration into the estate of the former Harrogate Arms Hotel.

Opposite: Borders in summer at RHS Harlow Carr. (Copyright RHS Harlow Carr)

Sequah

A little below where today's Beulah and Cambridge Streets meet, there once stood a line of cottages which were fronted by a piece of land that for some reason was given the colourful name of the 'Italian Gardens'. This was the favoured pitch of Sequah, the travelling sensation and one of nineteenth-century Harrogate's most colourful personalities. He was a tall Yorkshireman of around thirty-five years of age,

Beulah Street site of former Italian Gardens.

Sequah – photograph by
Grossman. (Courtesy of the
Wellcome Collection CC BY)

possessing long black shining hair, an aquiline nose, and high cheekbones, given
to wearing a costume of heavily tasselled buck skins, a gaudy neckerchief and a
high-crowned, wide-brimmed grey floppy hat. Sequah claimed to be a North American
tribesman with special power to cure people of their ailments – gout, rheumatism,
indigestion, toothache – with his 'Prarie Flower Oil', which was guaranteed to banish
any illness, no matter how long-standing. This became so successful that it made its
inventor a very rich man. Sequah was also known for his 'painless dentistry', which
he performed on those people who had never consumed 'Prarie Flower Oil'.

   Sequah lived the itinerant life of a traveller, living in a gaudily gold-leafed caravan,
who operated atop a platform mounted on a wagon, which was drawn through
Yorkshire by a horse, with Sequah announcing his presence by banging a large drum.
When he arrived at his favourite pitch on Beulah Street's Italian Gardens, Sequah
could gather a crowd around his wagon by the power of his oratory. To accompany his
'painless dentistry' sessions, Sequah hired a military band, who stood in a semicircle
around the wagon. Sufferers from bad teeth were then called upon to step up to the
platform and sit in the chair, their mouths open as wide as possible. At a signal,
the band then struck up as loudly as they could, and Sequah, forceps in hand, would

Above: An attractive display at Spirit of Harrogate. (Copyright Spirit of Harrogate)

Left: Spirit of Harrogate on Montpellier Parade.

examine the patient, and at an exceptionally percussive musical passage, extract the offending tooth. Extractions were carried out at the rate of two a minute, without any anaesthetic, the noise of the band and the applause of the crowd drowning out the cries of the patient.

Rheumatism sufferers were asked to seat themselves behind a screen that was erected on the platform, where they underwent a vigorous massage that was sometimes so effective as to enable crippled patients to walk away without their crutches – the relief no doubt being but temporary. When all the rheumatism sufferers had been treated and all the bad teeth extracted – a service for which Sequah never charged – the wagon would move away, accompanied by the military band, with Sequah banging his drum lustily. His real name was William Henry Hartley, who was so phenomenally successful that he ended up employing twenty-two other Sequahs. At his death in 1916, the *Harrogate Herald* published an obituary which stated that although he was reputed to have made a million in his lifetime, he had died in Johannesburg penniless.

Slingsby Gin

Yet another Harrogate success story. The Slingsby in question was William Slingsby, who in 1571 was the first person to recognise the important mineral qualities of the Harrogate Waters, putting Harrogate on the map as a world-class spa town. Spirit of Harrogate's range of spirits again brings that discovery to life. The unique quality of Slingsby Gin comes from the use of Harrogate Spring Water (itself a phenomenal success) and locally sourced botanicals, with twelve of these grown in Rudding Park's Kitchen Garden.

Spirit of Harrogate's first product, Slingsby London Dry, is a citrus-forward gin using grapefruit, and is created using twenty-four botanicals, all synonymous with the restorative nature of the town. The range, which is in every sense a Harrogate product, now has seven award-winning variants thanks to the avidity with which customers have taken to this superb brand. The company's range includes the popular Yorkshire Rhubarb Gin, made using rhubarb from the Rhubarb Triangle, and Gooseberry Gin, inspired by the crisp taste of a New Zealand Sauvignon blanc and created using delicious Yorkshire gooseberries.

Located on lovely Montpellier Parade, overlooking the famous Harrogate Stray, the Spirit of Harrogate flagship store and experience centre is decorated with its handsome bottles of varying colour, providing opportunities for eye-catching window displays. Visitors can discover the full range and development gins and book onto one of the experiences where they can learn about the history of gin, try different styles and make their very own personalised bottle. Slingsby's range is now being seen in more and more bars, hotels, airlines and retailers across the globe as it continues its barnstorming progress, ensuring that the name of Harrogate is carried around the world.

Standings

Although Standings closed as long ago as 1982, the author knows from countless conversations with older Harrogate residents that he is not alone in still regretting its passing. Standings, for those unfortunate souls who have no direct experience of pre-1980s Harrogate, was a splendid institution at the corner of James Street and Station Square. The ground floor was a high-class grocery store, with the range and quality of stock that is today found outside London perhaps only in Northallerton's Lewis and Cooper's, but on a far bigger and more impressive scale. The basement had a smoke room café, where gentlemen met regularly to enjoy tobacco and play chess. On the first floor was the large restaurant, which had splendid views of both James Street and Station Square. This was run by a trio of formidable waitresses, who would shout orders through a service hatch to the kitchens above. One of them was named Millie, who had pebble glasses and was quite unflappable. Getting a cup of coffee was something of an ordeal, as her shaking hands invariably ensured that most of the coffee ended up in the saucer. Several eminent spa doctors from the Royal Bath Hospital also used to meet in Standings, where they discussed the latest developments with some animation. Grocer Edward Standing had opened his business in 1883, when it soon became the leading grocery establishment in Harrogate, with a fleet of delivery boys on bicycles, and an imposing commissionaire at the front doors, who held them open for any customer known to have an account there. Such was his success that he was able to turn it into a private limited liability company on 1 February 1894, but shortly after this, declining health caused Edward Standing to retire to Frome in Somerset, where he died on 10 October 1915.

Standings in 1911.

When the author first knew it, Standings was full of huge mahogany counters behind which were assistants dressed in long aprons. It was considered unthinkable for customers to help themselves, as the usual practice was for customers to be offered a chair from which the willing assistant was told what goods were wanted. The idea of customers having to carry a basket round the premises, or standing in a queue, would have been considered an appalling decline of service. When in its full Victorian splendour, Standings restaurant was 'oriental' in style, with a mass of stained glass, fretwork inlaid with mother-of-pearl, and little brass tables, but this was lost in around 1930 when the store was 'modernised'. Distinguished customers in the post-war years included Arthur Lowe, Harry H. Corbett, the Beverley Sisters, Diana Dors and Donald Campbell.

Far greater change occurred in the 1960s when the store lost its way and introduced self-service, which radically changed its atmosphere. Then, in what some may consider to have been the worst decision in Harrogate's business history, Standings was closed down in 1982, 100 years after it first opened and just on the verge of the change of taste that eventually saw the rise in demand in Harrogate for high-quality provision retailing, cafés and restaurants.

Standings Oriental Café.

Stray

The Stray, which is perhaps Harrogate's greatest asset since the decline of the taste for Sulphur Water, consists of around 220 acres of open grassland that curves round the heart of the town on the west, the south and the east. It was created in 1778 when the great Royal Forest of Knaresborough was sold, an action that meant that the once open royal lands, to which all had unimpeded access, could be privatised and closed for public access. Such closure would have prevented the public from visiting Harrogate's celebrated mineral wells, all of which arose on forest land, a result which would have been catastrophic for the community's economy. Recognising this danger, Parliament set aside land to remain forever open and unenclosed, the land containing all the known mineral wells then in regular use. The spaciousness of the Stray also provides space for bodily exercise, which the eighteenth-century medical profession recognised was a necessary adjunct to health. During the Victorian age, the authorities began to plant trees around the Stray's perimeter, which today contribute so much to the Stray's beauty.

The Stray's surface pasture was originally kept down by means of the so-called 'Stray Gates', imaginary gates that could be purchased by a strictly limited number of people who were then allowed to graze a prescribed number of animals on it – cows, sheep, and horses – whose grazing kept the herbage down to manageable levels. From the start of its life, the Stray became very popular, so much so that parts of it were worn away by pedestrian and vehicular traffic, which meant that those who had purchased 'Stray Gates' had less herbage for their animals to graze. To compensate for this loss caused by the appearance or roads and footpaths, Parliament passed a second Stray Act in 1789, which created the so-called 'Stray-slips', whereby land parallel to the turnpike roads leading to the Stray, and equal in amount to the land lost to the roads and footpaths, was designated Stray. In the quiet times before motorised transport, cows and sheep could safely graze the grassy verges. The 1789 Stray Act established the important principle that has been respected by all subsequent Acts

In spring, the Stray is awash with colour.

of Parliament relating to the Stray: namely, that the Stray's surface herbage may be taken for use as footpath or roadway, but that the amount taken must be compensated by awarding a similar amount of herbage in return. Moreover, such new herbage must be as convenient to the public as the main Stray. In recent times, one of the loveliest features of the Stray is seen in spring, when its fringes are awash with colour from crocus, daffodils, cherry blossom, and wild flowers, of which dandelions, daisies, speedwell and, above all, buttercups provide delight to the eye.

The answer to the common question 'who owns the Stray?' is that it has two owners. English monarchs have since 1399 been the absolute owners of the Stray's subsoil, through right of the Duchy of Lancaster inheritance. The surface herbage however, was given to the people, and administered originally by the 'Stray Gate Holders', who were bought out in 1893 by Harrogate Borough Council, who ever since have administered

Spring wild flowers on South Stray.

the Stray on behalf of the public. Unquestionably, it has been this dual ownership of the Stray that has ensured its survival. What is often not grasped, however, is the fact that only an Act of Parliament can take away royal ownership once it has been established *by* an Act of Parliament. In effect, this means that land taken to build roads, etc. does not cease to be Stray land once the herbage has been removed, but is still Duchy of Lancaster property. Consequently, it cannot be returned to the Stray as 'compensation' for fresh loss of herbage because it never ceased to belong to the Stray.

But regardless of the legal aspects of the Stray legislation, the simple fact is that the general public has been Stray's most effective protection. The twentieth century in particular saw several attempts by the authorities to use the Stray for whatever currently fashionable activities were in vogue, such as conference centres, exhibition halls, multi-lane highways, hula-hoop enclosures, boating lakes or parks, all of which were said to be essential for the progress of Harrogate. But the public would have none of it, knowing that the best way of ensuring Harrogate's progress is to leave the Stray as it is, and to obey the age-old mantra 'Hands off our Stray'.

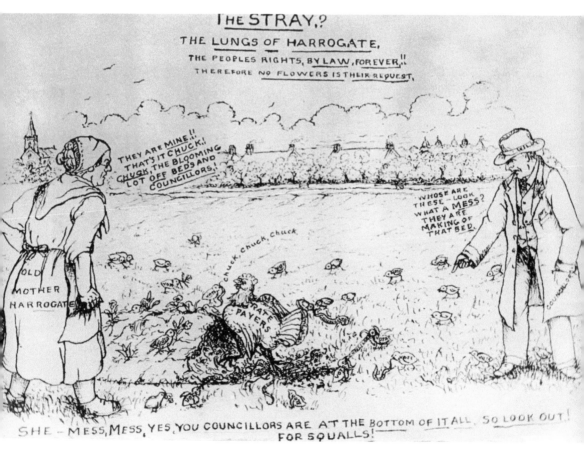

Battle of the flower beds – Old Mother Harrogate and a councillor.

Tewit

Here is where it all began – Harrogate's spa. It was in 1571 that William Slingsby identified the mineral water that flowed to the surface here as being identical to the waters he had consumed at the celebrated European resort of Spa. The much-repeated story tells that Slingsby was riding through the royal forest when he alighted to refresh himself by a wells. The waters reminded him of those at Spa, so he informed his acquaintance, Dr Timothy Bright, who visited the spot and confirmed Slingsby's opinion. Dr Bright, who had attended Queen Elizabeth, spread news of this discovery, which was taken up by the medical profession with enthusiasm. When in 1626 Dr Edmund Deane published his book on the Harrogate Waters, he recorded that Dr Bright had, in around 1598, coined the happy name 'The English Spa' for this well, which is the first ever recorded use of the word 'spa' as applied to anywhere in England. This makes the Tewit Well England's oldest spa.

The name Tewit is a north country word for pewit, large numbers of which used to flock around the open well to peck the encrustations of salts created by the mineral-rich water, although this died out after the well was protected and a public pump installed. Classed as an iron, or chalybeate water, it was always recommended for cases of parasitic infestation, and also as an antidote to anaemia. The pump room, in the form of an open Roman temple whose dome is supported by twelve Tuscan columns, originally stood over low Harrogate's Old Sulphur Well, where it was erected in 1807–8 to a design by Thomas Chippindale, but with the building in 1842 of the new Royal Pump Room, the older temple was dismantled and rebuilt at Tewit Well, a protective wall being added, with an attendant to dispense the waters from within. Those who did not wish to pay the entrance fee could drink the waters from a free outside pump.

For exactly 400 years, England's oldest spa enabled visitors to drink the celebrated waters of the Tewit Well, until an incredible act of stupidity by Harrogate Borough Council and its modernising Town Clerk ordered its closure in 1971. Subsequently, the pump was removed and the pipes to the well head, which lay a little to the south-east of the Pump Room, abandoned. Today, even the exact location of the mineral well that made Harrogate has been lost, although the pretty little temple that once sheltered pilgrims to the waters still stands in a quiet corner of the south Stray,

Low Harrogate's Old Sulphur Well received its characteristic cupola in 1808

Above: Thomas Chippindale's 1808 Cupola over the old Sulphur Well.

Below left: The Cupola, rebuilt in 1842 over the Tewit Well.

Below right: The Tewit Well Cupola today.

perhaps dreaming its dreams of the days when Betty Lupton, 'Queen of the Well', dispensed the life-giving waters to all and sundry who came to drink from the source of Harrogate's success.

Toffee

Harrogate Toffee, the name of which can conjure up the very essence of a wonderful lemon and butter flavour, was originally invented in 1837 by a Mr Robert Swan, a grocer, for the express purpose of countering the nasty taste of the water from the town's Old Sulphur Well. He left his recipe to Mrs Ann Farrah, who had assisted Mr Swan in his shop, and it was Ann, together with her husband Joseph, who was said to have improved and perfected Mr Swan's original recipe. The business seems to have been continued by the Farrah's from the premises behind the Crown Hotel, which stood only a few feet away from the Old Sulphur Well. At first production was limited, but in 1840 it began on a regular basis. Following the death of Ann Farrah in 1843, Joseph married Esther Varley, and in 1849 their son John Farrah was born. John went on to build up the business, registering the Farrah trademark in 1887, and on 16 February 1897, the company of John Farrah Ltd was created, one year after John Farrah had disposed of the business. John spent his last years living at a country farm before his death in 1907 at the age of fifty-eight. It is John's signature that appears on the famous blue tins that to this day can be found in shops all over the world.

In 1901, the directors of John Farrah Ltd acquired new retail premises at No. 7 Royal Parade, paying £3,750 for the property, which they converted into a ground-floor shop

Farrah's Montpellier Parade premises. (Copyright David Hodgson, Farrah's of Harrogate Ltd)

Display of superb
handmade
chocolates
at Farrah's.
(Copyright David
Hodgson, Farrah's
of Harrogate Ltd)

with living accommodation above. By 1997, Farrah's managing director was Michael
Waddington, whose retirement led to fears that the historic business would close
down. It was however saved by Gary Marston, a successful Harrogate confectioner
who moved Farrah's retailing from Royal Parade into his own premises on lower
Montpellier Parade, which he renamed 'Farrah's'. In addition to its incomparable
toffee, Farrah's also produce fine-quality fudge, nougat, biscuits and preserves, and
their displays of hand-made chocolates are at the heart of their beautiful shop. Today,
Farrah's Harrogate Toffee – under the control of Peter Marston – is as famous as ever,
even though the waters of the Old Sulphur Well have fallen into neglect. Throughout
the years since its creation, Farrah's Harrogate Toffee has won high praise from
all over the world. In 1910 it was awarded the gold medal at the Japanese-British
Exhibition, and nearly ninety years later, in 1998, received the ultimate accolade of a
visit from the Queen, who had first tasted the toffee as a child, when her father had
brought a tin from Harrogate in 1937.

The Queen at
Farrah's factory
in 1998.

Unikum

Although many people think that spa treatment consisted of visiting a pump room to drink a glass of mineral water, or possibly immersing themselves in a bath of it, the reality was that at their peak spas could offer their patrons a wide variety of treatments, which in terms of the medical knowledge of their time were at the

HARROGATE ROYAL BATHS.
An Inhalation Room.

Inhalation Room, or Atomisation Chamber, Royal Baths.

cutting edge. One such range of treatment was provided in Harrogate's Royal Baths, where an 'atomisation' or 'pulverisation' chamber enabled doctors to apply mineral water to affected parts of the body in whatever form was considered most efficacious. Just as today, a woman may apply an expensive cream to her body in the belief that its highly advertised oils and minerals are absorbed through the skin to positive effect, so did doctors of earlier times believe that the skin could absorb minerals present in mineral water. One method of doing this was developed to deal with disorders of the nasal tracts, the lungs and the throat. A special device would reduce the preferred mineral water to a fine mist, which could be administered to localised areas of a patient's anatomy via a fine tube or spray. The Unikum was one such device, which produced a very fine spray suitable for treating catarrhs of the lower parts of the trachea and lungs. The physician could order the water to be warmed and used with or without the addition of salts. Other methods were with the Duplex apparatus, which was fitted with a movable spray tube that could be inclined in various directions in treatments of the post-nasal space and larynx. The Solo was a fine vaporiser that used oils as well as waters, and was used to treat conditions of the pharynx. The Hochdruch was a powerful atomiser that was worked with compressed air, and was more intensive than the Unikum. It had nozzles for the mouth and nose and was used to treat catarrhs of the nose and upper throat. Finally, the Thermo enabled medicament to be volatised by means of an electric bain-marie. The medicated and filtered air was then inhaled through a valvular mouthpiece.

The Unikum and its related treatments were provided in a specially designed room, which was octagonal in shape, fully lined with magnificent tiles, and fitted with single booths to accommodate the different treatments and their patients. Today, the room has been splendidly restored by the Royal Bath's Chinese restaurant.

Valley Gardens

Before the Great Award of 1778, every square inch of Harrogate belonged to the Crown through the Duchy of Lancaster inheritance, but in 1778 when the Crown sold off much of its land, the area of the present Valley Gardens was divided between the various bidders for the freeholds – apart, that is, from a triangular-shaped field that contained many of the then known mineral wells, which because of its public importance was

Valley Gardens entrance flower beds *c.* 1925.

designated part of Harrogate's Stray. The mineral wells had converted the field into a kind of marsh or bog, which gave rise to the name 'Bogs Field'. Visitors wanting to reach Bogs Field used a footpath across land held by the vicar of Pannal, which ran from Bogs Field to the famous Old Sulphur Well and the Royal Pump Room. Over the decades, the footpath became well used, and after the 1841 Harrogate Improvement Act created the Improvement Commissioners, one of their earliest Acts was to embellish the footpath with plantings. Gradually, the authorities added more land around the footpath until in 1886–7 they felt the time was ripe for a competition to lay out the whole area as a landscaped garden. From that time to the present, the Valley Gardens have matured and developed, although the percentage of land devoted to formal flower beds has been reduced since 1974, when the reform of local government meant that resources had to be spread across the entire Harrogate District, including Boroughbridge, Knaresborough, Masham, Pateley Bridge and Ripon.

The first building in Valley Gardens was erected in 1858, when the Improvement Commissioners built a pretty little pump room for the popular magnesia waters. Designed in the Gothic style, the building was beautifully restored by the Friends of Valley Gardens in 2015 for use as a museum and educational centre. The success of the 1858 building was so great that in 1895 it was replaced with a larger pump room –

Beneath the Sun Pavilion's art deco dome.
(Copyright Harrogate Convention Centre)

one of the prettiest spa buildings of Victorian England – that now contains a splendid and much-frequented café. After the First World War, Valley Gardens received further embellishment in the 1920s when the tennis courts, children's boating pool, Japanese Garden, and Bogs Field circle flower beds were laid out. The 1930s saw the building of the Sun Colonnade and art deco Sun Pavilion, whose superb ensemble along the northern boundary of the gardens was very nearly lost in the 1990s, before being restored by the Friends of Valley Gardens to such a high standard that it was reopened by the Queen in 1998. Another object of interest is the New Zealand Garden, created in 1954 to commemorate Harrogate's ties with that country, and the twenty-three New Zealand airmen who had been stationed in the town during the Second World War and who had lost their lives in the conflict. The present New Zealand Garden was rededicated on 12 August 2010 after a careful and thorough programme of restoration. Further evidence for the public regard for Valley Gardens came in 2018 with the restoration of the Japanese Garden (which was reopened by the Japanese Ambassador) and the erection of the Edward VII Peace Gate on Valley Drive.

The combination of beautiful trees, shrubs, flower beds, buildings of architectural excellence and a pervading air of tranquillity make Valley Gardens an essential part of any visit to Harrogate.

Japanese Garden in 2019. (Copyright Jane Blayney)

Official opening of the Edward VII Peace Gate. (Copyright *Harrogate Advertiser*)

Victoria Avenue

There is perhaps no better place to view the sloppy conservation policies of the last century towards Harrogate's incomparable Victorian townscape than Victoria Avenue. This handsome and broad thoroughfare, with its many fine buildings and magnificent trees, was the creation of the Victoria Park Company that was established in 1860 by Richard Ellis and the Carter brothers to connect the two ancient villages of High and Low Harrogate by an imposing avenue that would set a standard for the further urbanisation of the town. Initially, the company brought in George Dawson's architect, J. H. Hirst of Bristol, to lay out the estate and plan its roads, but after slow take-up of plots, builder Richard Ellis himself bought many of them, and oversaw the construction of more and smaller structures than had been originally planned by Hirst. Ellis also increased the natural beauty of the avenue by donating the grass verges, the great circular garden of Victoria Circus, and the many trees that are the avenue's principal feature.

By the time of the First World War, Victoria Avenue had reached the full perfection of its creator's vision, the great stone villas being largely occupied by the professional classes, of which the spa's doctors were predominant. Each of the grass verges, together with the wide pavements, were provided with railings and gates to which

Victoria Avenue's chestnut trees in full bloom.

the residents had keys, and the grassy central strip formed a pleasant promenade that ran from West Park to Queen Parade. The parking of vehicles of any kind was absolutely forbidden, as the road had been built for the passage of moving rather than stationary traffic. At night, illumination came from lovely ornamental lamp standards, which were furnished with brackets from which flower baskets were hung in summer, with each lamp standard ringed by small circular gardens planted with colourful summer bedding plants. Only the empty site of the planned Town Hall at the junction with Station Parade remained unrealised.

The degrading of Victoria Avenue began in 1941, when to instil the population with a sense of contributing towards the war effort, the government ordered local authorities to organise the collection of salvage, including gates and railings. As the greater proportion were made of cast iron, their recycling for Spitfire manufacture should have been questioned, and the majority ended up as scrap. Victoria Avenue's

Victoria Avenue with intact railings *c.* 1900.

splendidly elaborate railings were entirely lost between 1941–4, and in 1954–5, the beautiful standard lamps were replaced with concrete posts that Sir John Betjeman described as 'looking as though they were being sick'. At the same time, the flower beds encircling each lamp post, together with the hanging baskets, were removed, and orders given to cover the central promenade with 'bitumen and limestone chippings' to accommodate increasing numbers of motorists who, presumably, were too lazy to park in the corporation's car parks. The devastation increased during the 1960s and 1970s, with no fewer than five handsome Victorian villas and apartment buildings demolished for replacement with the ubiquitous shoeboxes that were spoiling so many other towns. To add insult to injury, the absurd one-way traffic flow of 1968–9 turned Station Parade into a racetrack, requiring the second of Victoria Avenue's geranium-filled roundabouts to be swept away in a move that effectively split the avenue into two sections. More recently, and thanks largely to the uncaring North Yorkshire County Council, the concrete lamp posts have in their turn been replaced with motorway-type masts, and some of the pavements covered with a black tar-like substance that is so indistinguishable from the road surface that it is probably the reason why so many cyclists mistake it for the highway.

But there is still hope for Victoria Avenue. A few public-spirited owners have restored several lengths of railings and gates, some of the avenue's finest buildings have been cleaned and are once again in residential use, and Harrogate Civic Society has encouraged the replanting of trees where obvious gaps had been allowed to develop. But for Victoria Avenue to realise its potential as one of the UK's most recognisably Victorian streets, and a popular magnet for film and TV crews, as well as tourists, much more needs to be done: the railings should be restored throughout the length of the avenue; the pavements should be flagged with traditional Yorkshire stone and properly maintained; the vile lamp masts should be replaced with posts and globes of traditional Victorian appearance; the parking of cars should be completely banned (Victoria Avenue was built for *moving* traffic and not to accommodate abandoned vehicles); the central promenade should be restored and grassed over, and on the freed-up space, new cycle tracks provided. Finally, the road surface should be fitted with traditional Victorian stone sets. Achieve all this, and Victoria Avenue will become one of the wonders of the nation.

Victoria Avenue's superb mansions.

W

Woods

Wonderful Woods, also known as Woods of Harrogate, is Harrogate's oldest business. In a town whose attractions conjure up so many superlatives, it is particularly challenging to do justice to Woods, a name that is celebrated by the discerning across the globe as a byword for quality and attention to the needs of its customers.

Once known as Woods Linens, this unique family business has its origins in a 1733 Mercer's business in Laugharne, South Wales, which towards the end of the century operated from the historic Knaresborough flax mills, where present owner William Woods' great-great-grandfather first wove fine linen over 200 years ago. Linen shops could once be found in many major centres of population, but with the advent of cheap foreign imports and synthetic fibres, they dwindled, and today, Woods of Harrogate is the last such speciality shop in the United Kingdom. Properly maintained, a piece of Woods linen will last several lifetimes and improves with age, which is why Woods has so many eminent names as customers. Today, however, although Woods' range of linen and cotton goods is still breathtaking, the firm is

Woods of Harrogate. (Copyright Nicholas Richardson)

internationally famous for its work with interior design, work which can include the refurbishment of a single room or an entire property, the only matter common to both being the highest expectations of the client.

Woods' first Harrogate shop was opened in 1895 in Princes Street, by William Woods' grandfather, whose meticulous attention to the needs of his customers became established as being at the heart of his business. It was this, together with the knowledge that no better quality of goods could be had anywhere, that led to customers returning time after time. By 1926, the business had outgrown its Princes Street premises, and moved into more spacious accommodation at No. 67 Station Parade, part of a larger terrace of handsome properties that had been put up by James Chippindale in 1895, and provided with a magnificent canopy of cast iron and glass. Over the decades, Woods expanded into neighbouring premises at Nos 65–69, and in 1992 contributed generously to a plan by Harrogate Civic Society to enhance the whole terrace of properties, which was renamed as Prince Albert Row. Woods' shop windows are celebrated for their breathtaking displays, which rival anything in London's Bond Street. In all truth, there is nowhere like Woods of Harrogate. The place is simply unique, and is the very essence of what makes Harrogate Harrogate.

A Woods of Harrogate interior display. (Copyright Nicholas Richardson)

X

X-rays

Harrogate acquired a set of X-ray equipment shortly before the First World War, when it was installed in the Royal Baths. This was a little before the appointment of Fred Broome at New Year 1915 as managing director of Harrogate's Wells and Baths Department, whose dynamic administration introduced many scientific innovations relating to hydrotherapeutic treatment. The Royal Baths reported such success with their X-ray equipment that in 1912, the town's Education Department asked if they could borrow it to treat children infested with ringworm, a request denied by the busy Royal Baths, which forced the Education Department to purchase their own equipment. X-ray equipment appears to have been used principally with diagnostic work, but according to the *Sheffield Independent* in 1914, Rontgen Rays were being used at the Royal Baths to administer combined light and heat treatments, alongside the older forms of electric light and ozone treatments, and the Dowsing Radiant Heat Bath.

The next innovation were the Simpson rays (essentially ultraviolet radiation), their use in medicine coming from an observation by an electrical engineer named Simpson whose assistant suffered from eczema. Mr Simpson noticed that when the assistant used an arc lamp with Wolfram electrodes (a tungsten ore) the eczema was cured. At first, the Simpson rays, or 'S' rays, were inefficient burners, but were improved after the use of pure tungsten, when they became proper tungsten arc lights. The S rays were probably at the peak of their popularity from 1916–17, when Harrogate Corporation sanctioned their installation at the Royal Baths. By April 1916, the local Harrogate press was reporting that the older 'X' ray process used in medical photography was 'absolutely indispensable at the Harrogate baths'.

Not all of the local medical profession were in support of the adoption of new treatments at such short notice. Harrogate Medical Society, at their meeting in February 1916, expressed support for Fred Broome's intention of adding new apparatus for the static electricity treatment, and also for improvements to the peat massage treatment. But they asked the Wells and Baths Committee to defer the installation of the Simpson light. Here, the Harrogate Medical Society was at variance with the Wells and Baths Committee, whose attitude seems to have been that if a rival spa got something before Harrogate, so much the worse. The Royal Baths played second fiddle to none!

ARTIFICIAL ULTRA-VIOLET RADIATION 57

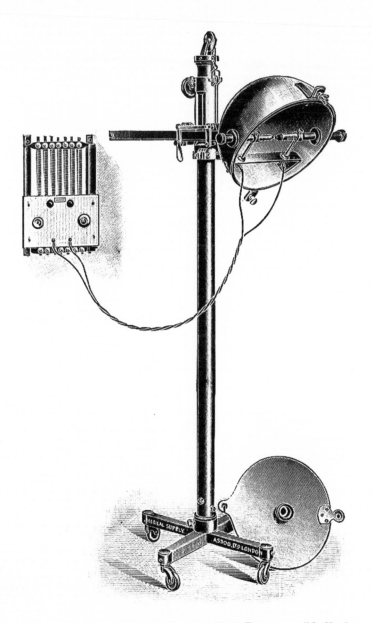

FIG. 14.—Tungsten Arc Lamp—Hall Pattern. (Medical Supply Association.)

Simpson Ray equipment *c.* 1915.

Y

Yorkshire Farmers Meat Company

Undoubtedly one of Harrogate's top retailers, the Yorkshire Farmers Meat Company is a shining example of how a business can survive amidst a changing market without lowering its traditional high standards. Back in 1936, when Ernest Robinson founded the business in Beulah Street, the Harrogate trades directory listed fifty-one independent butchers in the town, including Addyman Dearlove at No. 1 Eastville Terrace, Mary Bulmer at No. 10 Westmoreland Street, Benjamin Rushforth in Bilton Lane, and Yorkshire Farmers at No. 11 Beulah Street. Knaresborough had eight butchers listed, with four at Starbeck. Today, and disregarding the big supermarkets, central Harrogate has no butcher with bigger premises, a more comprehensive range of carefully resourced, stored and displayed stock, or a larger number of expert staff than Yorkshire Farmers.

Yorkshire Farmers Meat Company premises. (Copyright Yorkshire Farmers Meat Company)

Shortly after the end of the Second World War, the completion of Harrogate's new indoor market hall provided Fraser Dickinson – who had taken the business over from Ernest Robinson – with the opportunity to access larger premises, where the company enjoyed rapid expansion with local customers revelling in their ability to buy the best locally sourced, high-quality meat products. However, the redevelopment of the Market Hall in the 1990s meant that alternative premises had to be found, and the firm moved into lower Beulah Street.

The lower Beulah Street premises thrived so much that Fraser's son Mark and his business partner Mark Skinner, who by then had become managing directors of the company, moved into larger premises at No. 37 Beulah Street, wonderfully located at the junction of both Beulah and Oxford Streets. This had, by 1907, become the Harrogate branch of the Argenta Meat Company, and the building had a long tradition with the sale of high-quality meat products. But there is more to Yorkshire Farmers than the high quality of its produce. Thanks to the dedication of the staff, and their obvious concern for customer satisfaction, every visit to Yorkshire Farmers is a pleasant experience for customers. The place has a character and atmosphere all of its own, and one enhanced by the eye-catching attractiveness of its displays, which emphasise the local origins of many of its meats. Staples such as beef, lamb and pork are naturally well represented, but Yorkshire Farmers' range of stir-frys (the duck stir fry is outstanding), pies (try the magnificent chicken, mushroom and bacon with its golden pastry covering), including pork pies of such succulence as to ensure the author's reluctant travelling great nephews, Finley and Hamish, gladly undertake the lengthy car journey north on the *express* understanding that a Yorkshire Farmer's pork pie or lamb shank awaits them on arrival. The range of seasonal game is outstanding (try the partridge) and less common ranges such as goat and venison should not be overlooked. All things considered, an invaluable part of a Harrogate shopping experience.

Mark Dickinson and Mark Skinner – Yorkshire Farmers Meat Company.

Z

Zeta-Alpha

Zeta-Alpha was the government's top-secret name for Harrogate that was adopted shortly after the selection of the town as a location for various departments of state evacuated from London at the outbreak of war in 1939, and also during the subsequent blitz on British cities. The existence of so many large hotels and public buildings made Harrogate an obvious home for the Air Ministry, the Ministry of Aircraft Production and the Post Office, as well as units from the RAF and Women's Auxiliary Air Force.

Harlow Manor Hydropathic, Harrogate.

RELIABLE SERIE

Harlow Manor Hydro, home to 500 Air Ministry staff by 1940.

Crown Hotel.

Of these last two, the most significant sections were the No. 7 Personnel Reception Centre, the headquarters of the Medical Training Establishment, the WAAF depot, and the RAF section of the Air Ministry. Along with London accents, the sound of American, French and Polish voices became common in Harrogate as the war progressed, as indeed did the various accents from all parts of the Empire, particularly those from Canada and New Zealand. Harrogate also became a refuge for many children sent to Zeta-Alpha to escape the bombing campaigns. The Empire, of course, played a huge role in the defeat of the Axis powers, and without the Empire, the UK today would probably have been a Nazi fiefdom – something the critics of Empire would do well to recall.

Cold Bath Road had a high number of evacuated Ministry departments throughout the war, with the Wellington Hotel occupied by the staff of the Ministry of Aircraft Production, the Adelphi as a Personnel Reception Centre for the Empire Pilots Receiving Scheme, and the now demolished Harlow Manor Hydro by the Air Ministry.

The imposing frontage of the Hotel Majestic. (Copyright Hotel Majestic)

A little further away, the Hotel St George was occupied initially by the Pensions Department of the General Post Office before the Air Ministry moved in, also occupying the Crown. The huge Hotel Majestic was eventually taken over as 'Personnel Reception Centre no.7', where no less than 850 sergeant pilots were accommodated. Despite the secrecy of the move, it was not long before the traitor Lord Haw-Haw revealed all the addresses of evacuated government departments over the Nazi radio network. However, the Harrogate hotels had the last laugh, as it was a future manager of the Cairn Hotel, Captain Lickorish, who, on active service, participated in the capture of William Joyce, whose sneering tones had earned him his derisory name of 'Lord Haw-Haw'.

Acknowledgements

The author expresses his gratitude to the following for their kind co-operation with the writing of this book: Bilton Conservation Group and Warren Considine for images on pages 53 & 54; Jane Blayney for images on pages 82 & 83; Councillor Nick Brown for images on page 50; James and Nicky Cain and Harrogate Spring Water for images on pages 34 & 35; Sharon Canavar and Harrogate International Festivals for the image on page 25; Cardamom Black and Nick Rahmon for the image on page 22; Farrah's of Harrogate for images on pages 76 & 77; Jean MacQuarrie and the *Harrogate Advertiser* for images on pages 6, 31 & 83; The Harrogate Club for images on page 14; Mark Dickinson for the image on page 91; Harrogate Convention Centre and Simon Kent for images on pages 44, 45, 61 & 81; Mark Hinchliffe for access to The Chapel and to Alex Telfer for images on pages 12 & 13; Mike Hine for the image on page 15; Hotel Majestic for the image on page 95; HRH Group and Simon Cotton for images on pages 21 & 22; International Gilbert & Sullivan Festival for the image on page 24; Peter Jesper for images on pages 38 & 39; Vik Lokie for generously providing the author with access to his fine collection of historic postcards; Mercer Art Gallery for the image on page 20; John Nelson and his daughter Samantha for access to the Coach & Horses; Robert Ogden and Ogdens of Harrogate for images on pages 55 & 56; Pinewoods Conservation Group and Neil Hind for images on pages 57, 58 & 59; RHS Harlow Carr Gardens for images on pages 63, 64 & 65; Mark Skinner for the image on page 91; Anne Smith for the image on page 29; Nicholas Richardson and Woods of Harrogate for images on pages 87 & 88; Spirit of Harrogate Slingsby's Gin and Rebekha White for the image on page 68; The Wellcome Collection for the image on page 67; William Woods for images on pages 87 & 88; Yorkshire Farmers Meat Company for the image on page 91.

If the author has failed to thank any other contributor, he apologises for his unintentional oversight. Copyright acknowledgements are provided with the image captions, those with no accreditation being copyright of the Walker-Neesam Archive.